"Jo Ann's impact on the community is undeni⸳¹ ⸳ ty she mentors, her friends and colleagues, the ⸳ 'r family, and those who she touches through h ⸳s book opens the door for others to do the same. ⸳ ⸳⸳n, for sharing your personal story and reminding us all abou⸳ ⸳ne importance of personal purpose and leading with the heart."

—DANIELLE PORTO PARRA,
Chief Marketing & Digital Officer

"Sometimes we all need to reflect a bit and get refocused on the right things. Jo Ann Herold's amazing book, *Living on a Smile,* warms the heart while making you think more deeply about your purpose, passion, and the power of being more human. Jo Ann's storytelling, tremendous sense of humor, and keen insights kept my attention and I often caught myself alternatively laughing and being moved by her words. If you want to read a book to help you be a better servant leader and a better human, read *Living on a Smile!*"

—RANDY HAIN,
Husband, father, executive coach, president of Serviam Partners and author of
Essential Wisdom for Leaders of Every Generation

"Want to have more joy and success in your life? Read this book! Written by a true servant leader, you will learn how to smile more, be happier, and lead a bigger, more meaningful life."

—KEN BERNHARDT,
Regents Professor of Marketing Emeritus, Robinson
College of Business, Georgia State University

"There is no one on this planet more qualified to write a book called *Living on a Smile* than Jo Ann Herold. Jo Ann's positivity is infectious, her zest for life is genuine, and her energy knows no bounds. In a world where challenges are everywhere, Jo Ann sees them only as opportunities. It's always a good day when I'm around Jo Ann."

—BEN DEUTSCH,
Board Chairman, Covenant House Georgia/ Former VP, Corporate
Communications, The Coca-Cola Company

"Jo Ann is known in the community as a leader who builds amazing teams and lives her life by following her heart. Reading this book gave me a better appreciation for how she has been so successful—in life and business—by leading with heart, purpose, and that infectious smile."

—JEFF HILIMIRE,
CEO of Dragon Army, Co-Founder of Ripples Media,
The A Pledge, 48in48, and Ripples of Hope

"Jo Ann speaks to her audience with an authentic voice about what's in their heart—every page brought a smile to my face."

—DAVE SUTTON,
Author of Marketing Interrupted

"Jo Ann Herold is a dear friend to so many because she exudes joy and has a genuine interest in helping others thrive. This book will get heavily dog-eared and notated by most readers because it is a clear "how-to" guide to being happy and fulfilled. In *Living On A Smile*, Jo Ann has generously shared the people, principles, and path that impacted her and can now guide you."

—JOE KOUFMAN,
Founder & CEO, Setup

"I have had the privilege of having Jo Ann Herold in my world for about 30 years, first and foremost as a friend and also as an occasional professional collaborator. Jo Ann's life and life's work have been guided by passion, collaboration, and by being authentically present. The wisdom she shares from her own experience, and from those who have made an impact on her, are proof points of the love and respect she brings to every encounter as a light, a spark, and a bad ass."

—LOUISE MULHERIN,
Communications consultant, Savannah, GA

Living on a Smile

16 Ways To Live A Big Life And Lead With Love

Jo Ann Herold

First printing 2022

Book design by Najdan Mancic

ISBN 979-8-9859540-1-2 Paperback
ISBN 979-8-9859540-2-9 Hardback
ISBN 979-8-9859540-0-5 Ebook

Published by Ripples Media
www.ripples.media

For my parents, Marilyn and Mike Streiff, my brother, Mike, and my sister, Blake. To my husband, Mark, and my amazing daughter, Lily. To my inspiring group of family, friends, and colleagues who make life grand.

Contents

Foreword 1

Introduction 5

1. Passion Pizzazz 7

2. Purpose Planning 22

3. Planning, Pivoting, and Knowing When it's Time to Leave 44

4. People and Posse 54

5. Progress—Go For It, Go Get It 64

6. Personality and Play—Glow with Authenticity 82

7. Powerful Pursuit 91

8. Perspiration and Innovation 112

9. Positivity: Be a Positive Light in the World 121

10. Pushing to "Yes And, And" 127

11. Playlists 136

12. Pathfinder—Good Goes Around 142

13. Purpose to Serve Others 151

14. Practice Joy, Feel Happiness 159

15. Pastimes and Legacy 170

16. Prepping for the Next 50 Years—26 Million Minutes 176

The (W)rap Up 184

Closing and Gratitude 188

About the Author 191

Other Titles from Ripples Media 193

Foreword

by Julie Bowerman

After reading *Living on a Smile* and contemplating the important task of writing this Foreword, I kept asking myself the question, "Where do I start?" There are many starts I could write. Jo Ann the accomplished marketer who made it to the top tier of roles that many marketers aspire to hold. Jo Ann the successful mom of an amazing teenage daughter who is heading off to college. Jo Ann the servant leader who has tirelessly given back to so many, always with a smile. Jo Ann the person of faith without judgment. Jo Ann, my bestie who has shared many a glass of wine with me, sometimes over tears, many times laughing. In the end, all of these are the starts. All of them are the traits, stories, and words of wisdom that *Living on a Smile* gives the reader.

As part of Jo Ann's "posse," I have had the special opportunity to see her in all these forms. Some people would call this "having it all," but what Jo Ann has distinctly done is define her purpose, set goals to achieve her purpose, and lived her life accordingly. As she shares her story with humility, you'll hear how that wasn't always the case, but she stayed in pursuit. She sought tips and guidance from so many mentors, peers, friends, family, authors, etc. The book provides a collection of this wisdom that is inspiring and worth every minute of reading.

Jo Ann's superstrengths are her optimism, courage, generosity, and humbleness. These traits are infectious when you are with her and it's why her huge network adores her. She's down to earth while polished, takes on new goals with determination, and is the first to lend a helping hand to a friend or human in need. She believes in the good of people, and I often hear her say, "We are blessed." These are the reasons why Jo Ann is not just successful professionally, but also successful in life.

I met Jo Ann when our daughters, Lily and Reilly, were three. They're now 18. We both had marketing careers with goals of achieving more and a shared commitment to being great moms. Through all the trials and tribulations of trying to do both, Jo Ann and I were each other's trusted advisors and dear friends. Our friendship quickly grew to "friends who are family," as Jo Ann would say. Our families have shared many of our daughters' and families' milestones along with the everyday events and celebrations. The memories are endless and will last our daughter's lifetimes. It is truly one of our greatest blessings, and I have benefitted as a result of all the good ideas, love, and experiences Jo Ann shares in this book.

Even though I've known Jo Ann for years and knew many of the stories in the book, I walked away from reading this book inspired and motivated to live my life a little more like my friend. So, with my copy of *Living on a Smile,* my *Full Focus Planner,* Value Cards, *Blue Zone Cookbook,* and a smile on my face, I know my life is a little bit more fulfilled thanks to Jo Ann!

JULIE BOWERMAN
Reilly's Mom, Chief Marketing and Ecommerce Officer at
The Kellogg Company, and Forever Bestie of Jo Ann

Foreword

by Kate Atwood

Okay, first of all. Congratulations to you! Be prepared to be moved and inspired, whether you picked up this book because you've known Jo Ann for a lifetime or because this is your first introduction to the feel-good executive.

Few women have had an impact on me like Jo Ann Herold has.

Jo Ann came into my life at a transformational time in my career. I had just joined the Arby's brand family to lead the Arby's Foundation. The brand was under new leadership, and our Foundation charter was under a new mission. This was a turnaround of all turnarounds.

To this day, it was the most challenging work endeavor in my career. It was also one of the most formidable growth periods in my career, and I owe a lot of that to Jo Ann. Here's the thing about turnaround teams. We are often the ones written out of the wiki page. We usually don't reap the monetary benefits of our successors. But the experience leads you to focus on what is most important in a happy life: the people, the attitude, the perseverance. Because of Jo Ann, her principles and values, and her support and guidance, my chapter at Arby's became one of my most fulfilling.

A favorite quote of mine from Maya Angelou reads: "I've learned people will forget what you said. People will forget what you did. But people will never forget how you made them feel."

You can't talk about Jo Ann without talking about how she makes you, and everyone, feel. To experience her love and light is stuff that legacy is made of. Every time I see Jo Ann, to this day, I am greeted with a big hug and smile.

Throughout this book, Jo Ann gives colorful accounts of others who have achieved great success and from who she has drawn inspiration. Read them all. Soak them in. This is our chance to get inside the mind and heart of one of the most intentional and empathetic leaders of our time. As you read, remember, only a lens with love could write an entire book capturing the essence of others.

I want you to read this book to understand the level of presence, kindness, and genuine desire to care it took to capture these moments with such detail.

So, let's take a moment to raise a glass (of chardonnay, of course) to the one and only Jo Ann Herold. To the fierce energy and the righteous intention that has carried many of us through trials and transitions, alongside celebrations of success. And for those of you who are just meeting her for the first time through these pages, welcome to the fan club.

KATE ATWOOD
Founder of LoCo+ and Kate's Club

Introduction

This book is a celebration of my mentors. I celebrate the family, friends, colleagues, neighbors, and strangers who inspire and surprise me daily. Through love, laughter, sweat, tears, grit, grace, and amazing experiences, I've observed and collected the wisdom from those who've guided me through life. The people I'm here to celebrate gave me the courage to pursue a challenging life, a fulfilling career, and a center balanced by purpose and love.

To whoever is seeking answers or asking the questions themselves, this book exists as a conduit for the wisdom of inspiring people. Sharing their sage words is my way of honoring the profound impact they have had on me.

I am perpetually curious about what makes successful people tick and how to apply these behaviors to my daily life. As you read their stories, I hope you become inspired in a way that speaks to you. This lifetime of observations is ordered (to my humblest ability) chronologically, so that you may experience the rhythm of what I've learned along the way, about leading with love and mentorship.

My affinity for observing myself and others paid off in spades. Time is a most precious resource. Throughout the book, enjoy prompts that ask you to dig deep. May they bring forth your fullest happiness, the kind that slows time.

This book has some of my "GoGo's" (personal "to do" lists) at the end of each chapter. The ditties are a creative expression at the end of each session. One of these days, I am hoping to have a rap session encompassing the ditties. We'll see, but they were fun to write!

1

Passion Pizzazz

Do what you love, love what you do.

Dressed in red and yellow polyester, my career began. I was in high school working as a STAR at McDonald's. I had the honor of starring as the Hamburglar, which was notably ironic considering my squeaky clean rap sheet. STAR at McDonald's is an acronym for Store Area Representative, which sounds stiff, but meant we got to entertain children at the endless birthday parties that came through the store. It was warming to make people happy by being exactly what they needed. Had you asked me then, I wouldn't have guessed this job would set the path for my career. I learned two valuable lessons from this experience.

One, I love serving others. Food is the ultimate source of joy. The franchisees who owned the restaurant instilled a strong work ethic around showing up early and staying productive. Essentially, how to build the foundation of good service.

Two, I have an enduring love for consumer brands' ability to connect people to themselves and others. Brands are people and the people behind the brand are what makes strong connections.

I was hooked, so I decided to be the STAR who went for it. As full circles go, two decades later I wrote my master's thesis on McDonald's. No, it wasn't a biopic on the Hamburglar, but an exploration of my fascination by the brand's bursting emergence in China. Starting a supply chain in a new country was only the beginning of their pioneering brand's force.

A force so strong that even today, every road trip my husband and I take involves a McDonald's cheeseburger and fries. My frontline experience at McDonald's propelled me into roles with The Honey Baked Ham Company, LLC; Arby's Restaurant Group; Interface; and back home to The Honey Baked Ham Company, LLC. This lifelong career all began with passion.

"What if I fall? Oh, but my darling, what if you fly?"

— ERIC HANSON

The concept of Roots and Wings is essential for my passion's vitality. I believe if you have real roots grounded by strong values and positive people, you can soar. Roots, like a tree trunk, are filled with a quiet, deep, unyielding strength.

I grew up on the Mississippi Gulf Coast, where a sense of place and purpose is a part of the culture. A stunningly beautiful spot on the bayou, Ocean Springs is located between New Orleans and Mobile, off Interstate 10. It's a place where everyone knows your name and will often treat you to the best shrimp po'boy or escargot in the world. Ocean Springs looks a bit like New Orleans' Canal Street, Laguna Beach, California, and Savannah, Georgia all wrapped into one stretch of home. Ocean Springs is where I feel most at home. Every December 26, at 4 p.m. on the dot, Susan, Becky, Katy, Tina, Angie, Debbie, Patti, and fingers-crossed Maureen, show up to talk about the future, but mostly end up laughing as we reminisce about high school days. My friends and family are my roots and my wings.

MARK AND LILY

I met my husband Mark in Jackson, Mississippi, through a big circle of friends. When Mark moved to Chicago, I thought I'd never see him again. Serendipitously, we reconnected in Georgia and have been together ever since—30 years to be exact. Mark is a go-getter, a great man, and a wonderful father. Lily is our teenage daughter. She's such a wise spirit and lovely person. I can't wait to see how she guides her life using some of the principles I'll be sharing.

MOM AND DAD

Mom and Dad were high school sweethearts in Gulfport, Mississippi. She went to Catholic School, excelling in education, and he attended public school, excelling in math and high school football. Dad earned a computer science degree at Mississippi State—the first class to ever have the option of a computer science degree! He was hired to work at Boeing after college, joining a team among the first to put a man on the moon. My mom and dad are my roots and wings. My mom has brilliantly bright turquoise eyes. She's smart and beautiful, a powerhouse who loves her family, her church and her friends. She taught kindergarten and third grade, fueled by her own love of learning. She's an expert chef who grows her own veggies and catches crabs from the pier to make crabmeat au gratin (or the best crab cakes in the world when we're lucky). Family is the pinnacle of everything she does. My parents are at the core of who I am. They are my heart, my soul, my conscience guides. The love and guidance they've instilled within me are best told through stories.

BUZZ AND THE JELLYFISH

My dad has always been curious and funny. He adores his friends, believes anyone who likes to fish is a good person, and worships his family with genuine kindness. His love for dogs is a close second due to the uncanny connection he builds with every dog he meets. I was certain I'd eventually catch him speaking "dog."

Growing up, we adopted a lot of animals; cats, hamsters, bunnies, and chickens all had their place in our little zoo. When my brother and I were quite young, we would fish with Dad on Davis Bayou and try to sneak home the live bait, usually a small shrimp or a worm, we were keen on admitting to our menagerie. We went so far as to name the bait until it was tragically hooked and traded for the grubby nibble of a fish. Mom mirrored our love for pets and was often the primary caretaker, or zookeeper in some instances.

While many pets lived among the Streiff household, there was no animal more beloved by Dad than Buzzsaw. Buzz, as we called him, was a bloated, gassy chocolate Lab with a jawline that went for miles. Buzz descended from Chainsaw (his dad) and

Jigsaw (his mother). Buzz's siblings were also named after saws. Their names ventured into obscure territory. Buzz lived the life. He often ran free with the family's dogs who lived at the end of the park. He was clearly the self-appointed leader of his pack of rag-tag neighborhood dogs. An ass-kicker among the canines, Buzz demanded respect.

My dad was Buzz's best friend and vice versa. They would fish and drink beer and Buzz could even pop a beer in his teeth and guzzle it like a drunken sailor. Dad'll tear up to this day if he talks about that dog. My parents had a long pier outside their house where they kept crab traps. Dad and his soulmate checked them everyday—the eve of May 16, 1994 was no exception. After it loomed under the surface awhile, Dad pulled the trap from the murky, bayou water and emptied the contents onto the pier. All kinds of crabs and sea life were freed only to promptly scatter, sending Dad chasing after them with a bucket.

Buzz could not resist the platter of sea bounty before him. He inspected each one until he came across a helpless, but unfortunately very alive, jellyfish. After a quick, approving sniff, Buzz slurped that sea nettle as if it were a prized delicacy offered up from the ocean gods. For all his intents and purposes, it was an oyster on the half shell decorated with roe. From the periphery, Dad witnessed the episode screaming tardily, "No, Buzz, don't do it!"

The jellyfish stung Buzz's throat as it went down, causing him to convulse and pass out. Dad was horrified. It had happened in the blink of an eye. He quickly responded by retrieving the jellyfish from Buzz's throat and giving him "mouth to snout."

He could be heard by a neighbor crying, "Please don't die, Buzz, please don't die." When his lifesaving attempts failed to bring Buzz back, Dad had to act fast. Kay Baggett, a long time neighbor, was a marine biologist, he thought, already running to her door like a bat out of hell. Kay followed him to Buzz's limp form. She pulled out a container of milk and poured it into Buzz's exasperated throat. Suddenly, Buzz woke up, threw up, and proceeded to act as if nothing had happened (except for the celebratory, spread-eagle jump into the byyyy-you). It was rumored that later the same evening, Buzz was seen guzzling a beer.

ACCIDENT PRONE

Blake, my sister, is ten years younger than me. She has three degrees and is practicing as a nurse, nutritionist, and general health expert. My younger brother, Mike, is just shy of two years my junior. He earns his livelihood as a bank president and spends much of his free time volunteering, but he played like a wild man as a kid. Growing up, I was the people pleaser. Mike, who has never been known for his subtlety, would host tantrums in Bill's Dollar store wearing camper shorts and cowboy hats. I remember him beating his head on the floor just to get a ride on the mechanical horse outside. Naturally, we would all cave and let him ride. It's funny to think about why we say "no" and why we can't stand being told "no."

Back then, there was no such thing as bottled water, Purell, or car seats. Lacking all the security measures we have today, it is amazing we are still alive. Mom had this dark green, brand new Monte Carlo—the cool car back then. One steamy hot summer day in 1970, we were driving to Fred's, radio blaring, windows down, with me in the front seat. I was five going on 10 wearing a dance recital outfit complete with a tiara, while Mike rocked his usual cowboy getup. We'd wanted gum so badly we were incessant about it. Finally, Mom handed me a piece of Juicy Fruit and seconds later Mike started wailing for his piece.

Briefly turning away from the wheel, Mom handed him a piece of gum. The rest is blurry, probably because we were a green blur blending into the pastoral on either side. The car finally stopped spinning and swerved into a ditch where it became stuck. We were rattled, we were shaken, and the impact it made on our memories is clear even to this day.

A man stopped to help and pushed the car out of the ditch. Still shaken, we started driving home. I began to scream when I looked out the rearview mirror to see someone chasing the car. Mom looks out of the same mirror only to see Mike running behind the car with a bloody head. Later we'd learn that when the car hit the ditch, Mike had flown out the open window like a champagne cork. Mom had been in such shock she didn't realize he'd been ejected. If you've ever seen the *Chucky* movies, you can pretty much imagine the scene. Flying out of the window required him to get a few stitches, but that fireball of a stuntman was fine. I'm still convinced he's superhuman.

KIM AND THE SPIDER LADY

Growing up in Ocean Springs was idyllic. We lived on Nottingham Circle, a cul-de-sac in a subdivision where every street was named after one of King Arthur's knights. Summer days were spent exploring the woods, catching tadpoles and watching them transform into frogs, soft-shell crabbing on the beach, and waterskiing in Fort Bayou.

Most of the families who lived on Nottingham Circle had kids our age. We would play kickball while the sun was setting or descend into more deviant, teen behavior like smoking cigarettes where we wouldn't be spotted. Susan Jones, the next-door neighbor's daughter and I were like sisters. We drank Mad Dog and Miller Light ponies 'til the cows came home and later lived next door to each other while attending Mississippi State. Susan is one of those friends I might not see or talk to as much as I'd like, but when we do, we don't skip a beat.

My other Ocean Springs confidante was Kim Moreton. Kim was tall, beautiful, blonde with huge green eyes. She and I spent many days on her canoe in Fort Bayou, water skiing while dodging alligators, and exploring Horn Island collecting sand dollars between our toes and storing them in a fishing bucket to bleach when we got home (everyone was doing it). Kim and I also attended Mississippi State together as bright-eyed, bushy-tailed freshman roommates with a penchant for curiosity. Kim's grandmother, Annie, was a famous internationally known writer and photographer who once had her own float in the Macy's Thanksgiving Day Parade.

Back in her early days, Annie was one of the first seven stewardesses for Eastern Airlines. Dubbed as the "Spider Lady," Annie became one of the world's leading authorities on spiders. She was a longtime resident of Powhatan, Virginia, where she owned and operated the world's only spider museum. After she passed, she donated the museum and its contents to the state of Virginia. Her collection of spider photographs, thought to be the most comprehensive in existence, was donated to the Smithsonian Institute, and her collection of live spiders lived at Harvard University.

When Annie would visit us in Ocean Springs in her bright yellow station wagon, she would bring some of her favorites: tarantulas, scorpions, and various other suspicious-looking spiders in portable, see-through habitats. Freaky—but she always livened up our lives. We would scarf crabmeat au gratin (non-homemade this time) and champagne on her kitchen counter while making cheese pepper bread for a midnight snack. I did my best to stay out of view from the spiders, in case they fancied me their midnight snack.

Kim left this earth way too early and I hold onto these memories as fuel to keep our friendship as alive as it was on those perfect evenings. She passes through my dreams in delightful ways, making me miss her dearly. Annie and Kim were such beautiful, enchanting people. Their impact on my young life lends itself deeply to my adulthood.

ROLE MODELS

My family and Ocean Springs friends are my earliest sources of inspiration, but a long list of professional connections have impacted my growth.

When it comes to unparalleled passion, Kate Atwood is a person to know. Kate and I worked together at Arby's where we became fast friends. She's a creator, entrepreneur, and community leader whose commitment to community is contagious. At 23, she founded Kate's Club, a nationally acclaimed not-for-profit based in Atlanta that supports children and teens after experiencing the death of a parent or a sibling.

Kate has received numerous accolades for her work advocating for children. Her book, *A Healing Place*, summarizes the driving forces behind her determinations. As passionate as she is about Kate's Club, she made the brave decision to find her replacement for board leader and chose to continue working as a consultant. This is where I had the opportunity to meet Kate. Arby's hired her to redefine the Arby's Foundation's purpose. As a result of the successful assignment, Kate was then hired to lead the Arby's Foundation with the mission to eradicate childhood hunger. Kate and the Arby's team engaged local communities and raised over $15 million for the cause.

Kate left at the height of success at Arby's to work with Hala Moddelmog, who was the President of Arby's Restaurant Group from 2010-2013 and went on to become the CEO of the Metro Atlanta Chamber of Commerce and then President of the Woodruff Arts Center. Kate went on to lead a movement to help Atlanta grow to become a next-generation city and a top-tier location for emerging tech and creative talent. Through Kate's vision and tenacity, she launched THEA, the first-ever, city-based video streaming service that empowered Atlanta's independent content creators to be the storytellers of culture and community for the "A" around the world. Hear more about this initiative on Kate's TED talk, "It's Time We Reframe Grief for Children." She has been a guidepost in my personal trajectory through her ability to cast a bold vision and passionately turn that vision into successful programs and initiatives.

Another inspiration is Dan Hendrix, the long-standing chief executive officer at Interface, Inc. Dan has an impressive history of selflessness and when Interface's Australia plant burned to the ground, he immediately stepped in to help. Dan's primary concerns were the associates and his innumerable brave acts of kindness instilled tremendous loyalty within the Interface team. While the plant was being rebuilt, all of the associates were able to keep their jobs. During his continued tenure with Interface, he racked up 5 million Delta SkyMiles, wrote 27 million emails, and crossed the globe on 221 transcontinental flights to be with Interface colleagues and customers. Thanks to a recommendation from Lisa Lilienthal, Interface's PR consultant, I worked directly with Dan as his CMO. I feel blessed to have seen him in action.

The following are some of Dan's best quotes from his book, *Love to Lead*, that he handed out to his global teams:

"Hard Work and Luck. Most of what people call "luck" is actually the result of hard work. You can actually control your own destiny! So, have a positive outlook—people follow optimists. Take responsibility for your successes and your failures. Make your own opportunities. And take risks—lots of risks."

I follow Dan's advice and take lots of risks, but I take calculated risks. I've found it's smart to put ideas on paper and financially model the impact of the risks. When I do so, it creates "buy-in" from my cross-functional partners and also illuminates what the impacts of the decision will be.

"Serve and Lead. Servant leaders put service first and leadership second. It's both a philosophy and a practice. In my experience, people who are called to serve often make the best leaders."

Serving others is what leadership is all about. It's about helping others succeed and grow.

"Follow Your Passion. Find something you love to do and show up with curiosity and openness, even when it's hard."

This philosophy is at the heartbeat of who I am. If you do what you love and love what you do, work will never seem like a drudge.

"Develop Mentors and Sponsors. Having a sponsor is different from having a mentor—and you need both. A mentor is someone who has traveled a path before you and can give you advice and insight on your own journey. A sponsor is someone who can do all that, but is also empowered to stand up for you, to encourage others to help move you forward. A good sponsor is hard to find. Make that relationship a priority."

Amen to Dan for articulating the difference between sponsors and mentors. I treasure both, and work hard to keep the relationships thriving with both.

"Think in 3D. I gravitate towards people who are inquisitive—who look at a question or a challenge from more than one point of view and who bring me back something more than I asked for."

Thinking in 3D is such a powerful word picture. I love these people who go above and beyond and are excited about bringing new ideas and ways of thinking to the table.

"Seek Out Smart. Know where you excel and have the confidence to complement your expertise by surrounding yourself with people who are smarter than you."

Smart people are energizing. They are ones who like ideas at all angles and help make great things happen.

"Have Fun. Make fun a priority from the start. Be able to laugh at yourself and laugh with friends. Laughter reduces stress and lets everyone know that you have your priorities in order."

If it's not fun, why bother? Humor is a great way to make a tense meeting enjoyable and to break the ice.

"Make Friends at Work. Ray Anderson, Founder of Interface, always said that people who sweat together, stick together. You will spend more of your waking hours at work than you will at home, and people who work together share a common set of goals and a common destiny. That is often enough to strike lifelong friendships."

I work hard to make friends at work. I've learned that when I do, I look forward to going into the office everyday. Jobs are more enjoyable and satisfaction is higher when you have friends at work.

"Find Balance. Find a way to advance your career, but also have a private life that affords you downtime and time to spend with your significant other or your family. Integrating your work life, your family life and your spiritual life is a goal, and every day, your ability to meet that goal will change based on how you prioritize your time. You can define spirituality in a way that is meaningful to you—but it's the thing that gets you outside of yourself, allows you to slow down and focus on something bigger."

No one ever said in their final moments that they wished they had spent more time at work. Balance has helped me put my career into perspective. Career is very important, but it's not the only dimension of who I am.

You can also choose your boss. I have done that many times during my career. One of my closest friends, Julie Bowerman, is the current Chief Marketing and Ecommerce Officer at Kellogg's and prior to that, spent almost twenty years at the Coca-Cola Company. Julie is a big believer in choosing her boss. She said her favorite quote is from her father, Stan Smith who often shared the sage advice of, "Do what you love and the money will follow."

Stan's point was not that you will make a lot of money doing what you love (you might), but more so, when you do what you love, money is not the focus because you are so fulfilled.

GUIDE TO FINDING YOUR PASSION

1. When have I been the happiest?

_____

_____

_____

_____

2. What about that situation was great?

_____

_____

_____

_____

3. What gets me going in the morning?

_____

_____

_____

_____

JOJO'S GOGO

- ☐ *Do what you love, love what you do*
- ☐ *Keep at it, show up and never give up*
- ☐ *Don't be afraid to try new things and pivot as needed*
- ☐ *The world is small and the world goes around and around—you never know who you'll run into years later*
- ☐ *Be kind, be curious and always have fun*

LIL' DITTY

Do what you love and love what you do.
This is so important as you choose,
When you do that, you will never lose.
You'll never be working, which is the best.
Follow your passions, I can attest.

2

Purpose Planning

Jimmyisms.

Through my experiences observing and learning from family, friends, and colleagues, I realized I could use my energy for good. Doing good is what delivering purpose is all about. I was lucky enough to get this powerful message early on thanks to Dr. Jimmy Abraham, one of my first mentors, who led student recruiting at Mississippi State.

Working and volunteering as an Orientation Leader at Mississippi State afforded me one of the best summers I've ever had with people who have become lifelong friends. Jimmy was and still is the kindest, most humble person I know. He had so many lessons to live by that we dubbed them "Jimmyisms," which I still strive to live by today. Here are a few of my favorites:

- A yes means yes.
- Actions speak louder than words.
- Be a role model.
- Be a team player.
- Be not afraid.
- Being nice and kind are acceptable behaviors.
- Celebrate differences.
- Do things on time.
- Do what you say you are going to do.
- Do your best.
- Don't be afraid to dream big. Dreams really do come true, even when they seem to be shattered.
- Don't complain.
- Don't let anyone intimidate you.
- Don't take things for granted.
- Don't wait for friends to leave this earth before you give them a standing ovation.
- Evaluate yourself.
- Every day begins a new year.
- Failure is not fatal; success is not final.
- Give thanks for all you have.
- Have confidence in yourself.
- Have fun.
- It's no big deal.

▸ Just as you are looking at others, others are looking right back at you.

▸ Keep things in perspective.

▸ Lead by example.

During COVID, Jimmy pulled together Zoom calls with the Orientation Leader classes to connect our classmates from the last 30 years. His key messages during the Zoom call stuck with me. Jimmy challenged us to start thinking about our legacies by asking ourselves these key questions:

▸ "How do you build your legacy?"

▸ "What do people say when they hear your name?"

▸ "How will people remember you?"

Jimmy implored us to:

▸ "Look for the up-and-comers."

▸ "Love people to their full potential."

▸ "Give our entire heart."

▸ "Share love and grace. Teams that are drawn together by love, stay together."

PUT YOUR PURPOSE ON PAPER

Part of my work at Interface was uncovering and articulating the company's purpose and values: *Lead Industry to Love the World.* Thanks to the help of Joey Reiman, Katherine Wilkinson, Cathy Carlisi, Dolly Meese, and some smart folks at Bright House, along with our Interface team members Anna Webb, Jay Gould,

Dan Hendrix, and Katy Owen, we captured the essence of the brand and the culture of our employees and customers. It was a bold and beautiful way of thinking about how a company can deliver value to its shareholders while giving back to the world.

Interface captured the essence of its brand and purpose in such a beautiful way. This leads to me one of the most important things I've learned in my work—lead with love and do it with the people you love. That belief is what led me to return to The Honey Baked Ham Company, LLC, eight years after I had left. I love the company because of its relentless focus on the associates and our customers. It's a brand that is truly iconic and has a unique position in the marketplace.

YOU GOTTA GET TO KNOW JEFF HILIMIRE

Jeff Hilimire has been a right-hand man on my personal and professional journey. First of all, Jeff is one of the greatest people I know. A family man, he and his wife, Emily, have five children, two of whom they adopted from China. Jeff is an entrepreneur's entrepreneur. He started Spunlogic, the digital marketing firm, while he was still in college at UNC Charlotte, bootstrapping the start-up with a computer and some credit cards.

His first gig was to develop a website for a business in New Zealand and he jumped at the opportunity. Jeff and his partner Raj Choudhury had just signed a lease on a building when that business failed. With no other option except to make Spunlogic work, Jeff and Raj persevered and persisted. I am proud to say that Honey Baked Ham was their first customer who put them on the map! Spunlogic developed The Honey Baked Ham Company's first website. We signed the deal on the surface of the ping-pong table in their new office!

Jeff and his team went on to win bigger accounts like Coca-Cola, The Home Depot, and UPS. They ended up selling Spunlogic to a bigger firm, Engauge, and then selling it again. Jeff then founded Dragon Army, a purpose-driven digital engagement firm. The Honey Baked Ham Company has been a client of all three of Jeff's companies and the reason is because of Jeff and the talent he attracts.

Jeff is also a big believer in the power of purpose. His personal purpose is to *have an outsized positive impact on the world.* He's also the author of *The Crisis Turnaround, The 5-Day Turnaround,* co-founder of 48in48, Ripples of Hope, and The A Pledge. Jeff shows on a daily basis how he is living his purpose.

KAT COLE ALWAYS INSPIRES

Another person who I admire greatly is Kat Cole. Kat started her career as a Hooters girl, right out of high school. She took the job to help support her family and pay for college. She was quickly promoted into an executive role, which had her traveling the globe to open Hooters Restaurants—all by the age of 26! During this time, Kat also gave back to her community by volunteering at the Atlanta Mission and mentoring young women at the Women's Foodservice Forum.

Because she was traveling so much, Kat dropped out of college. A mentor of Kat's encouraged her to get her degree. But Kat being Kat, she was able to secure a recommendation from Ted Turner to gain admission to Georgia State's MBA program without a degree. After she left Hooters, Kat served as the COO of Focus Brands for over a decade. Kat has decided to repurpose the next chapter of her life, choosing to serve on boards, invest in tech start-ups, write a book, and accept public speaking engagements. I do know that whatever she chooses, she will be a star.

Kat's *Checking In* blog post titled "The Hotshot Rule" sank in deeply. So often, we are given chances and we play it safe. Kat's Hotshot Rule involves the regular practice of envisioning someone else in her seat, asking what they would do, then doing it!

The following are a few of my favorite Kat Cole quotes:

> ▸ "Don't forget where you came from, but don't you dare ever let it solely define you. Your truth is in your roots, but your past is not your anchor."

> ▸ "If you don't use your voice, there's someone behind you who will."

> ▸ "Focus on things that are small enough to change, but big enough to matter."

> ▸ "Success is mostly driven by how badly you want something and how well you partner with other people. It has to do with how hungry you are."

> ▸ "Have empathy, gratitude and respect for every position in the company."

> ▸ "I've learned to question success a lot more than failure."

> ▸ "When we get our sense of self from only one place, when something goes wrong and the inevitable happens, it can crush you emotionally, spiritually, and physically. So it's important not to believe you are defined by one place, one relationship or one thing, and to find ways to keep your sense of self strong."

> ▸ "I trust the next chapter because I know the author."

WHY I LOVE DOLLY PARTON

Although I've never met her personally, Dolly Parton is my hero. She exudes talent, kindness, and purpose. I encourage you to watch her documentary on Netflix. My favorite quote from her is "Figure out who you are. Then do it on purpose."

I love watching her rags-to-riches life story and listening to how her songs tell inspiring tales. She wrote the theme song to the film "9 to 5" while on set and strumming her acrylic nails together like she was playing with a washboard. This song and movie became an anthem for so many working women trying to get ahead, and earned Dolly two Grammy Awards and an Academy Award nomination for best original song.

LEADERSHIP ATLANTA: "THE BEST CLASS EVER" AND ONE OF MY TOP THREE EXPERIENCES

I had the good fortune to be a member of Leadership Atlanta 2012—"The Best Class Ever." I always thought that Leadership Atlanta would be something I needed to do, but didn't know how much it would change my life. After one of our weekend retreats a few of us met up for cocktails in a treehouse (that is a long story) and shared stories, songs, and a lot of laughter.

One of my classmates who made a lasting impact is Loretta Young Walker. Loretta is a badass. At the time she was the chief human resources officer at CNN. She's also a very talented singer. Something else that I learned from Loretta is her philosophy for getting ahead. She calls it the "PIE theory."

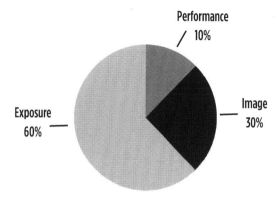

The acronym stands for Performance, Image, and Exposure and how important each one is for advancing to the next role. She encouraged young students to do the jobs no one else wanted to do and to stand out, be noticed, and jump in.

Another Leadership Atlanta classmate, Clark Dean, who is managing director and partner at Transwestern, is probably the most optimistic and fun person I know. That evening in the tree house, he recited Theodore Roosevelt's famous speech "The Man in the Arena".

> "It is not the critic who counts; not the man who points out how the strong man stumbles or where the doer of deeds could have done them better. The credit belongs to the man who is actually in the arena, whose face is marred by dust and sweat and blood; who strives valiantly; who errs, who comes short again and again, because there is no effort without error and shortcoming; but who does actually strives to do the deeds; who knows great enthusiasms, the great devotions; who spends himself in a worthy cause; who at the best knows in the end the triumph of high achievement, and who at the worst, if he fails, at

least fails while daring greatly, so that his place shall never be with those cold and timid souls who neither know victory nor defeat."

— THEODORE ROOSEVELT,

"The Man in the Arena"

IMPOSTOR SYNDROME

This is a fear of being discovered. I worry someone is going to figure out I am not good enough or feel like I shouldn't be in the room. I have felt way out of my depth and know others who have felt this way, as well. Have you ever felt this way? I've even heard that Matthew McConaughey and Rob Lowe have felt the impostor syndrome when they rose to fame and success.

According to *Psychology Today*, "People who struggle with impostor syndrome believe that they are undeserving of their achievements and the high esteem in which they are, in fact, generally held. They feel that they aren't as competent or intelligent as others might think—and that soon enough, people will discover the truth about them. Those with impostor syndrome are often well-accomplished; they may hold high office or have numerous academic degrees."

It's common for high achievers to feel this way. As a matter of fact, *Psychology Today* also states, "Around 25 to 30 percent of high achievers may suffer from impostor syndrome. And around 70 percent of adults may experience impostorism at least once in their lifetime, research suggests."

When I am feeling this way, out of depth or that I am swimming in the deep end, I remind myself that I must be doing something right, and to keep going, learning, taking risks, and acknowledging that I am supposed to be in the room or at the table. I am learning to take this fear to use it as a force for good.

PURPOSE PHILOSOPHY

I started studying purpose after I read Joey Reiman's book, *The Story of Purpose*. Many years after reading the book, I had the distinct pleasure to work with Joey and his team to uncover the purpose for Interface. Joey's book inspired me to study purpose and I learned about "ikigai," a Japanese philosophy on excavating your reason for being and having a meaningful direction or purpose in life. The philosophy says you are fortunate if you can find three passions you love: one to make you money, one to keep you in shape, and one to keep your creative juices flowing.

I had the privilege to teach as an adjunct professor for almost nine years from 2001 to 2010. I took the job mostly so I could study and learn academic ways of thinking from the best of the best and share it with people on my team. I will say that I learned more than I even expected, and it was one of the highlights of my career.

Smart frameworks help me articulate my thoughts. If it's not on paper, it's not a real idea. I utilized this Venn diagram to help illustrate my purpose.

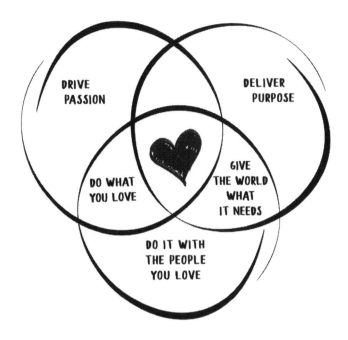

While ever evolving, this framework helped me define my purpose and put it on paper. I was a huge Covey fan, and used the Franklin Planner during the 80s, 90s and early 2000s, and I missed the art of writing things down on paper. Shucking my digital journals in 2017, I opted for Michael Hyatt's *Full Focus Planner* and started manually uncovering my purpose. It helps me from a lifelong perspective—as well as weekly and daily. Michael Hyatt has many free ways to help stay productive using his tools, that include video coaching, an online guidebook, and access to a private community.

Every day, I use my purpose to define how I want to live with kindness and gratitude, using a spot in my *Full Focus Planner* to list my big three goals for the day. Additionally, I write daily the things I am grateful for and what I've done to be kind to someone.

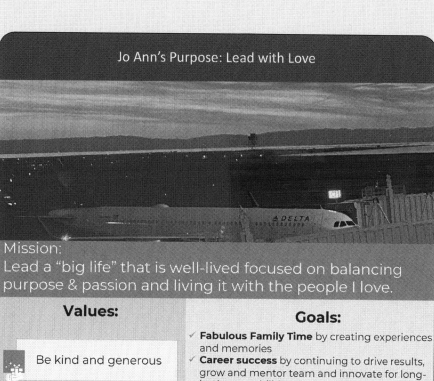

Jo Ann's Purpose: Lead with Love

Mission:
Lead a "big life" that is well-lived focused on balancing purpose & passion and living it with the people I love.

Values:

 Be kind and generous

 Over-deliver on the deliverables

 Drive lasting value. Leave a legacy

 Have fun, laugh a lot, show up and be there

 Take the high road and the long view

Goals:

✓ **Fabulous Family Time** by creating experiences and memories

✓ **Career success** by continuing to drive results, grow and mentor team and innovate for long-lasting capabilities

✓ **Cultivate relationships with friends** who are good for the soul

✓ **Exude joy & gratitude** by living each day as if it were the last. Do something kind for someone everyday

✓ **See the world** by creating a dream list of trips and putting them on the calendar

✓ **Listen & learn** by reading books, listening to podcasts, watching movies—all to gain knowledge

✓ **Make an impact** of my community by giving to causes that matter (Covenant House, Leadership Atlanta, AMA)

✓ **Show up and love** people to their full potential. Look for the up and comers. Show up and positively present by leading with love

✓ **Become an athlete** by continuing to run, play tennis, ride Peloton and identifying a sport for life

MY PURPOSE IS TO LEAD WITH LOVE. SO, WHAT DOES THAT MEAN?

▶ It's about trying to be a good role model for my daughter.

▶ It's about showing up for family events.

▶ It's mentoring someone on my marketing team.

▶ It's mentoring someone in the community.

▶ It's giving $20 to a homeless person I drive by on the street.

▶ It's overtipping for great service.

▶ It's buying someone's coffee at Starbucks.

▶ It's about only saying kind things about people.

▶ It's about letting someone go in front of me on the road.

▶ It's about holding the door open for someone.

▶ It's about bringing flowers and food to our elderly neighbors.

▶ It's about sleeping out and raising money for Covenant House.

▶ It's about doing a five-minute favor to introduce a college graduate to a company.

▶ It's about getting to know new friends in the gym and making a connection.

▶ It's about giving genuine compliments when I see something I like.

I started thinking about my purpose, putting it on paper, and articulating it. The first step was to write it down. Think about it for yourself and write it down. What is your purpose?

My mission is to lead a big life that is well lived, focused on balance and purpose, and sharing it with the people I love.

▸ It is about striving for my goals including travel, fun, exercise, and friends.
▸ It's about living each day to its full potential.
▸ It's about being kind and practicing gratitude.

Writing down your mission is the first step. I started by researching other people's mission statements, and digging deep into what is important to me. As you think about what is most important to you, start to verbalize what your mission is and put it on paper.

Once you have written your mission, it becomes somewhat of a touchstone on how to live your life. I read mine almost daily and make sure I am living up to what I've set out to achieve.

Values are the "golden rule principle" of behavior and judgment. My values are:

▸ Be kind and generous.
▸ Overdeliver on the deliverables.
▸ Drive lasting value at work.
▸ Have fun, be there, and laugh a lot.
▸ Take the high road and the long view.
▸ Be brave. Be a badass.

Here is a breakdown of my six values:

Be kind and generous. This value is about striving to be authentic with people and bringing my whole self to every situation. I work to speak out, to stand out, and to reach out. Being genuine creates a foundation for trust and deep relationships, investing in "we" over "me," and creating a culture of inclusion. I challenge myself to do the right thing, to be generous to people, and to the earth I call home. This is about doing the greatest good possible.

Overdeliver on the deliverables. This is about doing epic shit. I work, in all areas of my life, to exceed expectations, go the extra mile, make it stick, and drive positivity. I have a fire in my belly, I want to wake up the world to the power of possibility, for the greater good. When I am at my best, I am not only a light—but a spark that helps others catch fire. That light that lives in each of us, as we seek to light the way for one another, for our communities, our business, and for our globe.

Drive lasting value at work. This commitment is about leaving any place I work, or any volunteer leadership role I am committed to, better today than it was yesterday. Trust and excellence are about doing the right thing when nobody's watching. I am committed to making a difference, and leaving things better than when I found them. I am focused on excellence and evolving myself and my times through hard work and innovation—encouraging myself to learn, try new things, and grow.

Show up, have fun. This value has to be on my list. It is about being grateful to be alive and having fun with the people I love. Life is made up of minutes, moments, and memories. It's about enjoying small and ordinary pleasures. It's about living—really living. It's to be present and love the journey, not the destination. It's also about carving out the time to be there, committing to it, connecting, and having fun.

I take the high view and the long road. This is about letting things pass and looking on the bright side. It's about seeking the good in myself and others. And while I can't see every contour in my path, my purpose is my compass, and am confident on my trajectory toward a better future.

Finally, being brave, being a badass. This is about being confident in my point of view, realizing I am a diamond in the rough and also a masterpiece. It's about being humble, yet speaking out for what I believe in, what matters most, and what I am passionate about. It's about making progress and shining a light on things that can be improved.

Use this next area to articulate and write down your values. I write these down often and continually iterate and refine the wording. Anywhere from four to six values written down is a perfect place to start.

What are your top four to six values?

1. _____

2. _____

3. _____

4. _____

5. _____

6. _____

GOALS TO AIM TO A HIGHER RESULT

Goals can shift and change. Through the *Full Focus Planner*, I go through a regular cycle of planning annual, quarterly, and daily goals. My top 10 now are:

1. Fabulous family time.
2. Become an athlete.
3. Career success.
4. Friends who are good for the soul.
5. Exude joy and positivity.
6. Acknowledge gratitude and be happy.
7. See the world.
8. Listen and learn.
9. Make an impact.
10. Show up—what gets scheduled gets done.

I balance these goals based on the day of the week, but do spend time daily reflecting and prioritizing my goals.

What are your goals?

These goals will become very motivating over time. The most fun thing for me to do is write them down and then monitor progress. Recently, and at an older age, I've started to learn to play tennis. While I am not very good, I am making progress every week on the game and being able to learn a new skill.

Some of my favorite quotes:

- ▶ "Successful people are not gifted; they just work hard and succeed on purpose" —*G.K. Nielsen*

- ▶ "I've learned that people will forget what you said, people will forget what you did, but people will never forget how you made them feel" —*Maya Angelou*

- ▶ "Be silly. Be fun. Be different. Be crazy. Be you, because life is too short to be anything but happy!" —*Tinybuddha.com*

- ▶ "There are some people in life that make you laugh a little louder, smile a little bigger, and live a little better." —*Unknown*

- ▶ "For most of life, nothing wonderful happens. If you don't enjoy getting up and working and finishing your work and sitting down to a meal with family or friends, then the chances are that you are not going to be very happy. If someone bases his happiness or unhappiness on major events like a great new job, huge amounts of money, a flawlessly happy marriage, or a trip to Paris, that person isn't going to be happy much of the time. On the other hand, happiness depends on a good breakfast, flowers in the yard, a drink or a nap, then we are more likely to live with quite a bit of happiness." –*Andy Rooney*

- ▶ "Kindness is badass." —*Jo Ann's T-shirt from Amazon*

CAST YOUR VISION

A vision board is an effective way to share your goals. The first time I did one was when I was in the Leadership Pasadena class while living in California when we lived there in 1999. As someone just starting her career, it helped me focus on the goals that were vital at the time—career, health, family, travel, and saving for the future.

Starting a family was a priority and at the center of the vision board, which led to Mark and I adopting Lily, our beautiful daughter. Being the first person to hold her was the most poignant, indescribable experience.

Years later, Henna Inam, a whip-smart executive coach, led a few of her posse into a vision board party in Atlanta. She created a fun party, serving all kinds of delicious foods, and had old magazines that we tore swipes from to create our boards and then we shared them with others.

I still have both of these vision boards and it's crazy how many of the dreams on the board have come true.

GUIDE YOUR VISION !

1. What Drives Your Passion?

_____

_____

_____

_____

_____

2. Who Do You Like to Do It With?

_____

_____

_____

_____

_____

3. What Do You Love Doing?

_____

_____

_____

_____

4. What Do You Do Best?

_____

_____

_____

_____

_____

_____

_____

_____

5. What Are Your Strengths?

_____

_____

_____

_____

_____

_____

_____

_____

_____

JOJO'S GOGO

- [ ] *Look for role models while being a role model*
- [ ] *Surround yourself with people who love you for you*
- [ ] *Do things that matter—whether it's in your professional career or volunteer work*
- [ ] *Journal, meditate, and appreciate the simple pleasures in life*
- [ ] *Write down your values, your goals and your purpose, and create your vision board*

LIL' DITTY

Do things on purpose, cast your vision,
Follow your dreams, that is your mission.
Strong spirit and a humble heart is so lit,
You'll be too legit to quit.

3

Planning, Pivoting, and Knowing When it's Time to Leave

"Know when to hold 'em, know when to fold 'em, know when to walk away, and know when to run."

Kenny Rogers's song "The Gambler" is a song that runs through my head often. I had a young friend ask me for job advice and used the lyrics when we were problem solving on whether she should stay or go from her job. The song goes like this:

You got to know when to hold 'em,
know when to fold 'em
Know when to walk away, know when to run
You never count your money when
you're sittin' at the table
There'll be time enough for countin'
when the dealin's done

–KENNY ROGERS,

The Gambler

When I was 17, I decided to follow in my father's shoes and go to Mississippi State. I fell in love with the school and loved every minute of it. I think it's because of my love for the school and the people there—I got super involved on campus. Following in my mom's footsteps, I joined Delta Gamma (DG) where they modeled manners, making your grades, drinking beer from a cup instead of a can, and knowing how to circulate to percolate. I still smile when I think about Eleanor Slaughter, our advisor, lecturing us on acting like ladies and doing the right thing.

DG was not my first choice. I actually wanted to be in a different sorority, but that was not to be. I learned from that early disappointment to make the best of the situation, and to see the bright side. I decided to be the girl who went for it. The women of DG were big supporters of mine, and I was of them. They recommended me for Rush Counselor, Orientation Leader, Senate Leader, and Public Relations Chair, and then ultimately nominated and supported me running for Homecoming Queen. The Homecoming Queen campaign is tantamount to a political campaign. The DG's went door-to-door campaigning to get out the vote. I love them for it and still am in a group chat with many of my Delta Gamma friends, talking to them almost daily.

After Mississippi State, I entered the "real world." I did everything from selling copiers (not my thing) to becoming the Director of PR & Marketing for the Jackson (Mississippi) Zoo (which I loved). Regardless of the role, one thing was true—working as a young woman in the 1980s and 1990s, in a male-dominated field, was not for the weak of heart. I ended up working as a field marketing manager for a restaurant chain. As a 24-year-old young woman I was excited to have an opportunity working with peers who were in their 30s and more seasoned. I was excited about the role and it was a big step up for me in my career. Early in the job, we visited our ad agency in Atlanta. I was excited and nervous about such an important meeting with the leaders and experts.

The meeting went well and we all went to dinner after the meeting.

As I am writing this, I realized I've never told anyone that during this time, my boss's boss was visiting Atlanta. After one of our group dinners, he told me that the team was joining him in his room for an after party. Excited to be a part of the team, I went up to his room—only to learn no one else was coming. He tried to attack me. Fortunately, I was able to get out of the room before anything too bad happened. I ended up not saying anything to anyone, but could not ever look that boss's boss in the eye again.

I ended up being transferred to a better job within the company and was ultimately awarded with the Above & Beyond the Call of Duty Marketing Award for Captain D's.

I wish I could go back and tell my young self not to feel ashamed because of the boss's moves and that I didn't do anything wrong. I wish I could have told my young self to tell someone at the company. I wish I could hug my young self. Through writing this book, I think I did just that, as I am smiling through my tears.

The incident with the boss made me more aware and determined to do the right thing. Starting and finishing are what people remember the most—it's not always what's in the middle (unless you are an Oreo)! It's okay to want to move on and try new things. When there are more bad days than good days, it's time to move on. When it's time to try something new, do so with grace. Finish out all the projects and leave it where it's easy for the next person to come in and finish what you've started. I am one of the rare few who had a second career at the same first job. Good goes around and you just never know who you'll meet again later in life!

DEVELOP MENTORS AND SPONSORS

Nancy Gibson is on the top of this list. She was recruited to become HoneyBaked's chief marketing officer. I'll never forget seeing her on the *Today Show* being interviewed by Katie Couric on a new campaign that Diet Coke was airing. Nancy was a hot shot from Coca-Cola and knew the brand process and mining customer data like no one else. Nancy took a personal interest in me, and she and I became simpatico for over nine years. Nancy is still someone whom I seek advice from and try to grab dinner with every three months or so, and someone who became more than a boss, but a friend and role model.

Chuck Bengochea, HoneyBaked's longtime CEO, was also a boss and mentor. His expertise is finance and operations, and he coached me through working with him to better understand the numbers, being in the "foxhole" with my operations partners, and also how to better live a Christian life. By way of background, Chuck also spent a good chunk of his career at Coca-Cola and General Electric. He chose to work at HoneyBaked because of its strong values and good work-life balance. Chuck's philosophies are People, Planning, and Purpose. He used the framework to guide our strategic planning and to make sure that people were at the heart of our planning. Through his purpose, Chuck is now a motivational speaker and consultant, helping businesses design values-based cultures and truly lives out his people, planning, and purpose philosophy.

No one is better at planning than HoneyBaked's former CEO, Linda van Rees. She was mentored by Sergio Zyman, Coca-Cola's iconic chief marketing officer who believed that strategic planning aligned with conviction was the key to any business's success. Of all the places I've worked with, HoneyBaked is simply the best at planning. Linda is a zealot for quality and perfection within the brand. This commitment translates to a delicious product that is at the centerpiece of many important and emotional customer occasions.

SHOULD I GET AN MBA?

Because of personal goal setting, and the use of my handy Franklin planner, I had a goal to obtain my MBA. I wanted to round out my career and felt like I had more learning to do. As a result, I kept setting a goal to get my MBA and plotting it in the planner, but for some reason I kept procrastinating. Finally, I drove over to Mercer University, met with the dean, sat for the GMAT exam, and was admitted into Mercer's Executive MBA program.

I remember being so exhausted while I was simultaneously working on my MBA and working full time. It was like working a part-time job on top of my overly full-time job.

Did I need an MBA? No, not really. I was doing well in my career. People often ask me if an MBA is necessary to be successful in marketing or advertising. My answer is always—it depends on what your goals are.

Most small-to-midsize companies do not require that an entry-level marketing candidate have an MBA. In the marketing world, experience and hard work are the job requirements. Entry-level employees learn the ropes by getting in there and learning from more seasoned executives. It is critical in marketing to start at the bottom and work your way up. Time and experience are the only way to do this.

MBA graduates learn a lot about all functional business areas including economics, marketing, and finance. They learn quickly that the starting pay in advertising and marketing is not a good return on investment for their expensive MBA. There are a few good-paying jobs in blue-chip firms that require an MBA, but those jobs are few and far between.

I chose marketing and advertising as a profession since it's the most creative of any discipline in the business world. I am absolutely passionate about marketing and I work hard every day to be at the top of my game. I love that I am responsible for driving sales. It requires both art and science—the right and left brain.

This MBA has meant nothing and everything for me. It meant nothing in that I did not get a promotion or a raise as a direct result of earning the degree. However, what I did gain is a more global insight to the role of marketing and advertising, and how it impacts other functions and the organization as a whole.

I became a stronger voice at the table and was more confident in vocalizing my point of view. I was quickly promoted and given a raise because of the contributions I was making.

Another result of receiving my MBA was an invitation to be an adjunct professor at Mercer University. I have also been a guest speaker at numerous colleges and civic organizations. It helped me get promoted at HoneyBaked, go on to be the chief marketing officer at Interface, Inc., and VP of marketing at Arby's, Inc.

So, when I'm asked whether an MBA is necessary, I say it depends. If you are in marketing and advertising for the long haul and want a great career, I think an MBA will round out the business experience. It will also give you credibility, too. It is not a good return on investment in the short-term, but will definitely pay out in the end. As marketers will tell you, we are always looking to prove the return on investment. So, because of all that, the MBA has meant everything to me and I would emphatically recommend it.

CRITERIA FOR DETERMINING SUCCESS

Something I learned from working with a few bad bosses—and then some really strong ones—is that three criteria are necessary for success.

Criteria for seeking a new role or staying in a current position:

Do I believe in the brand or business?
1. Is this a business that has a unique position in the marketplace?
2. Do I believe in their values and purpose?
3. Is this work that I am excited about doing every day?
4. Is there a good culture?

Do I like my boss?

5. Is this someone I respect?
6. Is this someone I can work for and follow?
7. Is this someone I'd like to go to lunch or dinner with?
8. Can I trust them?

Can we be successful as a team?

9. Will we have the resources to grow?
10. Do we have support from the stakeholders?

If I can answer "yes" to all of these questions, it's usually a good fit and a good balance. If there is a "no" to any of these questions, things are out of balance and will not quite be working for me. Sometimes when there is a "no," I'll work out an arrangement to get things back in balance.

WHAT GREAT LEADERS DO

Great leaders set a beautiful vision, establish the values, enable decision-making, and keep the team focused. They are uncompromising on delivering value to their customers and are relentless about setting clear objectives for the organization and their teams and about knocking down barriers for the organization to grow.

Goal-setting and follow-through are key. Mostly, it's being able to spot what's working and what's not. I use this simple guide to help plan.

GUIDE FOR PLANNING

1. What are my three top goals for the year?

_____

_____

_____

_____

_____

2. What are my three top goals for this month?

_____

_____

_____

_____

_____

3. What are my three top actions to achieve these goals?

_____

_____

_____

_____

_____

4. What is stopping me?

_____

_____

_____

_____

JOJO'S GOGO

- ☐ *Find a tool to help you plan (*Franklin Planner, Full Focus Planner, *or any simple calendar that works well for you)*
- ☐ *Have goals and write them down*
- ☐ *Leverage mentors to help you reach your goals*
- ☐ *Keep learning, keep growing*
- ☐ *Do work that feeds your soul*

LIL' DITTY

Should I stay, should I go? Only I know.
Should I move up, move over or move out?
Look for signals, they are always about.
It's about doing nothing, or a change.
Advice from a friend or prayer help rearrange,
To provide clarity, when it's time to make a change.

4

People and Posse

A posse is a faithful band of friends whom you call during times of merriment, crisis, or adventure.

When Lily went off to school, I encouraged her to be nice to everyone—the teachers, all students, the bus driver, the maintenance team, coaches—everyone. I like to be friendly to all and have a wide variety of connections and friends. Friends are my escape and truly one of the fruits of life. My posse is a jolly, diverse tribe of men, women, elderly people, and children. I learn something from all of them.

Think through who is in your sphere. People with purpose, goals, and visions have no time for drama. They invest their energy into creativity, positivity, and doing good in the world. Friends have significant power over a meaningful life.

Dan Buettner, the *New York Times* bestselling author of *The Blue Zones Kitchen*, suggests changing your surroundings to set your life up for good choices. He mentions that your friends have long-term and measurable impacts. Buettner goes on to suggest proactively finding three friends who care about you on a bad day. He said having good friends is worth about eight years of your life. I have become a devotee of the "Blue Zones" way of living.

FRIENDS WHO HAVE BECOME FAMILY

There are career friends, people I love to volunteer with, and a group of friends my husband Mark and I have dubbed, "The Posse." We met "the posse" through our church and share a love of family, dance parties, good dinners, travel, and laughter. My husband Mark, Greg Bowerman, Eric Froseth, and David Clemons are besties. My fellow "Sassy Sisters" are Julie Bowerman, Karyn Froseth, and Donna Marie Clemons. Our children, Reilly, Hayley, Caroline, Dylan, and Lily are also great friends. It's a rarity to find couples and children who love being together. The Gryboskis (Stacy and Billy, Tom and Kasey) are also best friends. This posse is made up of friends who have become family.

My "Pasadena Book Club" has been there with me through thick and thin. Mark and I lived in Pasadena, California, for three years from 1998-2001. During our short time there, we met some of our best friends through my volunteer work with the Junior League in Pasadena. The ladies and our gents all have become tight. Even though I don't talk to this group every day, we manage to travel to see each other every year.

One of my favorite friends, Louise Mulherin, has been there for me every step of the way and has become a second auntie to my daughter, Lily, and a part of our family. Louise and I have traveled the world together, laughing along the way. Our circle of friends since the 90s, including Kevin Craft, Jim and Rosemary Hannan, Angie and Jon Naphin, and Steve Ethridge, have been there for each other during our most important moments. As a matter of fact, Jim and I worked together at Captain D's many years ago, and now he and I are working together again almost 30 years later!

MEET THE POSSE

Your posse isn't limited to family, friends, and close colleagues. For me, the many organizations I serve also have helped to build my posse. These include the CMO Club, the American Marketing Association (AMA), the GSU Marketing RoundTable, Delta Gamma, Leadership Atlanta, MSU Orientation Leaders and Roadrunners, the Atlanta Convention & Visitors Bureau, 48in48, Covenant House, the Junior League of Atlanta, and the Junior League in Pasadena.

Through the CMO Club, I've become friends with Danielle Porto Parra, a group CMO at Focus Brands; Melissa Minihan, head of Digital Commerce and Marketing at Veritiv; Jill Thomas, the CMO of PGA TOUR Superstore; and Kathryn Towns, the VP of Marketing for a private equity firm. We have a group text called the "Dynamic Dynamos" and our mantra is "Surround yourself with women who would mention your name in a room full of opportunities." Our friendship is easy, comfortable, and built on trust and loyalty. We have dinner, drink wine, and help each other out. As I write this, we are sharing photos of Melissa and her adorable new baby, whom we are already in love with. We're also trying to help Danielle recruit a VP of marketing for a non-profit, and generally just encourage each other through gratitude and wisdom.

From early in my career, I have admired and followed Dr. Ken Bernhardt. This guru of marketing created the Georgia State University Marketing RoundTable and wrote a monthly marketing column for the *Atlanta Business Chronicle*. I loved reading his articles and reached out to him. I broke a few rules from Sheryl Sandberg, and asked him to be my mentor the first time we met. Fortunately, Ken agreed, and continues to be someone whose opinion means a great deal. I volunteer, consult, and talk with Ken often.

Ken has been a consultant for Chick-fil-A for almost 40 years—the longest of all of their consultant relationships. I asked Ken what the best piece of advice he's received and he shared these words from his father, "If something is worth doing, it is worth doing it right. Always do your best. When you agree to do something, do it well."

One of Ken's favorite quotes is from Truett Cathy, the founder of Chick-fil-A, who said "Our goal isn't to get bigger. Our goal is to get better, and if we get better, we will get bigger." He also loved that Truett embodied the mantra "If you love what you do, you'll never work a day in your life."

Proverbs 22:1 states, "A good name is to be chosen rather than great riches, and loving favor is better than silver or gold." And Ken Bernhardt's name is gold.

Hala Moddelmog and Ken Bernhardt helped sponsor me to get into Leadership Atlanta. Leadership Atlanta encourages their students to build their power posse. There is a big group of us from the 2012 Leadership Atlanta class who serve on the board of Covenant House, a nonprofit that supports homeless youth. We are also there for our classmates who are appointed to be a judge, running for office, need to network for new jobs, or who lose a loved one. Leadership Atlanta has become one of the most significant networks I have. Being a part of the (best) class (ever) changed my life forever.

TRAITS OF SUCCESSFUL PEOPLE IN MY POSSE

I've been talking to a lot of people in my posse and doing some discovery on the traits of successful people. Over lots of coffees, lunches, and a few glasses of wine, I've interviewed these rock stars. The common themes are very compelling.

- ▸ They meditate or journal. Every morning they spend at least five minutes of time with themselves to figure out how the day is going to work.

- ▸ They are grateful and gracious. Some of them keep a grateful journal and highlight the top things they are grateful for each day.

- ▸ They don't waste a minute of the day. They know that their time is the only scarce resource and they make the most of every second, every day.

- ▸ They touch a piece of paper or an e-mail only once. They figure out what they need to do, deal with it, and move on.

- They do what they love and love what they do. They are passionate about their jobs, their avocations and they lead with purpose. They turn their job into a hobby and call it a "jobby!"

- They laugh a lot and look at their successes and failures as great opportunities.

- They are optimists who always look for the silver lining in every situation.

- They rarely eat a meal alone. They know that relationships are everything and work to have a coffee and lunch meeting with someone every day. Most of them are morning people and are big coffee drinkers.

- They love their families and friends and use the weekends to do fun things and spend time with the people they love. This brings joy and meaning into their lives.

- They are extremely present. These successful people put down their phones, listen, smile, and make eye contact. They show up, like to laugh a lot, and have fun.

- They exercise and stay in good shape knowing that exercise brings balance and clarity.

- They are gentle, kind, polite, and realize that being nice and kind are perfectly acceptable behaviors.

- They are curious by nature and big readers. They also love to meet people and figure out how they can help.

- They are authentic and bring their whole self to every situation. They take their work seriously, but not themselves. They are the "real deal" and what you see is what you get.

▶ They are wildly talented and add value every day. They deliver results in every aspect of their life. Whether it's leading a growth initiative at work, volunteering, or helping a colleague, they try to make their corner of the world a brighter place.

I find myself reading this list and checking myself against these standards and encourage you to do the same.

ON MENTORS

During my presidency at the AMA, we started a mentorship program pairing seasoned marketers with up-and-coming job seekers. We conducted a panel discussion with William Pate, the CEO of the Atlanta Convention and Visitors Bureau; Julie Bowerman, Chief Marketing and Ecommerce Officer at Kellogg's; Shannan Harlow; Steve Behm, the Southeast President of Edelman's; Dr. Ken Bernhardt; and Kate Atwood. The mantra for this mentoring panel was "Tell me who you run with and I'll tell you who you are."

The audience was interested in how to go about finding a mentor. Panelist Shannon Harlow suggested starting your search with people you admire. Julie Bowerman added that it's import-ant to have a few different types of mentors. Ken Bernhardt also advised that, when seeking a mentor, it's important to have people you trust to tell you the truth, like your own personal board of advisors. Ken added, when faced with difficult decisions, don't hesitate to ask for advice. Just like professional sports players have a coach, we all need a coach.

As it turns out, we can all be mentors. That means you can find a mentor in someone who already holds an advanced position in your career field, someone who is in a different career field you aspire to enter, college professors and other educators, or even someone who is just getting started but who you admire, trust, and who can give you solid advice.

Steve Behm reflected on a time when he received some great advice from a junior member of his staff and the importance of having a relationship with people at all career levels. Kate Atwood said, "Don't undervalue how powerful you, as a mentee, can be for a mentor." The experts explained that mentors should be humble leaders, have integrity and be willing to tell the truth with kindness, because as Steve Behm noted, "words matter."

Mentors offer examples of challenges and lessons that may help you find the answer in one of your own challenges. One of William Pate's biggest lessons learned was a time he almost got fired over an advertising campaign in the mid-90s for a product that integrated emails, fax, and pagers (oh my!). After the initial pitch, the CEO didn't like the campaign but William believed in it. He said to William, "I'll tell you what I'm going to do. I'll give you the money for it, but if it doesn't work, then you're fired." The campaign ended up being successful and William learned to believe in what you're doing.

If you don't have a mentor, seek one out and be available to mentor others. We can learn a lot from one another.

Warren Buffett may have said it best with this sage advice, "Surround yourself with people that push you to do better. No drama or negativity. Just higher goals and higher motivation. Good times and positive energy. No jealousy or hate. Simply bringing out the absolute best in each other."

GUIDE FOR BUILDING YOUR AWESOME POSSE

1. What do you like to do for service?

_____

_____

_____

_____

_____

2. As a volunteer?

_____

_____

_____

_____

3. Who in your posse inspires you?

_____

_____

_____

_____

4. Is there anyone who zaps your energy?

_____

_____

_____

_____

JOJO'S GOGO

- ☐ *Develop your power posse, nurture those relationships*
- ☐ *Friends and family are critical to "crushing it"*
- ☐ *Broaden your circle to volunteer and do good in the world*
- ☐ *Travel, have fun, laugh a lot with your posse*
- ☐ *Seek out people you admire and reach out to them. You never know who will be your mentor*

LIL' DITTY

The people around me make it more fun,
I'll never regret spending time when I am done.
No one wishes they spent more time working,
When you can be with your cherished ones.
Life is better with the people you love in the sun.

5

Progress—Go For It, Go Get It

Time is a scarce resource— use it wisely.

Whether it's writing a book, working a corporate job, or volunteering, making progress is critical. To make progress, you need process. Self-structuring will save you from stress, humanity's kryptonite. Worrying, complaining, or talking about how hard it will be can be replaced with sitting down, writing your outline, sharing it with others, and making it happen. This may seem like an "easier said than done" scenario but it's not! Tried and true, if you surmount the moment of fear in the act of starting, your process will bloom.

There are so many Stephen Covey quotes around this subject. I will share those that resonated most from my time as an early disciple:

- "Most of us spend too much time on what is urgent and not enough time on what is important."
- "Start with the end in mind."
- "Sow a thought, reap an action; sow an action, reap a habit; sow a habit, reap a character; sow a character, reap a destiny."
- "Live out of your imagination, not your history."
- "Seek first to understand and then to be understood."

More favorite quotes::

- "You may delay, but time will not, and lost time is never found again." —*Benjamin Franklin*
- "To accomplish our goals we must distill our dreams into daily action." —*Michael Hyatt*
- "Don't let good be the enemy of the best." —*Voltaire and every good leader I've worked with*
- "A winner is a dreamer who never gives up." —*Nelson Mandela*
- "The way to get started is to quit talking and begin doing." —*Walt Disney*

GOOD LEADERS AT THE TOP OF ORGANIZATIONS ARE LIKE ELITE ATHLETES

The best leaders are organized, visionary, strategic and excellent communicators.

▸ Excellent leaders are highly motivated and have an innate ability to serve others as well as uniting others into a greater mission. They follow a strict code of ethics.

▸ Excellent leaders have a strong work style and intensity to accomplish goals and tasks, while planning strategic work for the organization to grow top and bottom line sales.

▸ Excellent leaders build connections and relationships. They are highly effective in human interactions, and use their abilities to help others design and activate their success journeys.

▸ Excellent leaders have swagger and influence attitudes, actions, and behaviors at all levels.

▸ Excellent leaders have a clear thought process. They are strategic, understand a P&L statement, understand how to operationalize a concept and have vision.

LEVERAGE YOUR STRENGTHS, FORGET YOUR WEAKNESSES

When leading a team, it's important to understand the strengths of the collective team while simultaneously considering each individual's area of expertise. CliftonStrengths has been a tool and resource I've used at every role I've had. Talent matters in business and certain jobs require different skill sets. Understanding your own unique talents and the talents of others will help build natural strength. John Wells, the former president of Interface Americas, understood this very well. He developed a strengths-based culture at Interface and helped them grow their sales over $1 billion in revenues.

I've taken the CliftonStrengths assessment twice—10 years apart. It's based on Gallup data and I was impressed and surprised my strengths didn't change; a true testament of the tool's accuracy. When I started at Interface, we used the CliftonStrengths assessment to learn about each team member's individual strengths. It was smart because it's an inherently positive way to learn more about others using a disarming approach. We graphed and posted each team member's results and even included our strengths on our email signatures. My five strengths are futuristic, strategic, achiever, woo, and inclusive.

PERFECTIONISM, NO MAS

As a dreamer, I'm also a recovering perfectionist. This may sound strange because being a perfectionist is often considered a positive aspect, but I am working towards not being a perfectionist. As painful as it is, sometimes putting an imperfect framework or storyboard in front of the boss or the team is more beneficial for progress. Being relentless about making progress is showing results and bringing forward the plan or initiative without hesitancy. Providing simplicity and clarity in the midst of chaos is something I am very focused on.

When I started at Arby's, we did not have a product pipeline. Our new private equity partner, Roark, noted that when they bought us. Roark also funded Mattson, an awesome innovation partner in San Francisco, which enabled us to create some of the best work I've ever seen. Working alongside Barb Stuckey at Mattson was a game changer and as a side note, I hired Mattson when I was at HoneyBaked to overhaul our side dishes. I remember our lead partner from Roark, Steve Romaniello, saying to the team when we were debating whether to launch a product, "I would rather have a good product tomorrow, than a perfect product next year." It was great advice from a smart investor. I wrote it down and use this quote often. It was during this time that Arby's started showing strong positive sales and profitable growth.

POSITIVITY WINS

When I started as the new, global CMO of Interface, John Wells was so kind and generous with helping me learn a new industry. He would take time out of his busy day to go out of his way to teach and mentor. He, along with one of Interface's top sales people, Michel Belland, took time to share which areas would be beneficial for some of us to help with. Product development was an area where the business needed sales, marketing, and customer input. Working collaboratively with the team, we created an innovation calendar and an analytical approach to design and development, ultimately growing sales and profits for Interface.

Individual accountability and team accountability are crucial for success. John Wells created a collaborative, working relationship with sales, marketing, supply chain, and manufacturing to ensure customers were delighted and remained loyal.

Someone who exudes purpose and makes it happen is Randy Hain. Randy is the owner of a coaching practice named Serviam, and is one of my favorite mentors. He and I meet for breakfast every few months and catch up. Randy is one of the kindest people I know. He's one of those people who is always trying to think of kind things to do for others, such as giving them a book or writing a handwritten note.

A prolific writer and motivator, Randy often writes recommendations for others without them asking. He's given me countless books that are life changing. I am grateful to Randy for over a decade of friendship and dedication. He's a role model for me and many others.

Here's what I've learned from Randy Hain:

▸ Be kind to people, do nice things for them, but don't keep score.

▸ Expect the best in others. Let them know how much you believe in them.

▸ Get up early, do what needs to be done, and make it happen.

▸ Focus your day to help others and be positive. Ensure family time is woven in.

▸ Kindness is about lifting others up. It's not just an act, but a philosophy that you practice daily.

▸ Build your network, keep it alive, and don't wait until it becomes an emergency.

FAMILY ROCKS

My mom, Marilyn, is the best at making things happen. She loves to entertain, but she's not worried about making her dinner party for 50 perfect. For her, it's all about the people and the food, but she's not fussy about making every detail perfect. She also is a tech genius. She's the "go-to" for her family members when it comes to setting up a laptop, finding an obscure object, planning a non-profit event or a fun family vacation. She simply looks at the big picture and just does it.

While bragging about my family, my nice, Lindsay Streiff, is someone who had a goal to be a veterinarian since she was old enough to talk. She mapped out a plan, made excellent grades, and never took her eyes off the prize. She is now in her second year of vet school, and as she says, on her way to be a "DOGTOR." She certainly missed out on some of the parties in college while studying in her dorm room to reach her goal. In her pursuit for vet school, she earned a second degree in Animal Husbandry milking cows before daybreak to show prospective schools her dedication to her career choice.

MIRACLE MIKE

My brother Mike is 16 months younger than me and a great athlete. He played sports year-round. He was the winner of the Punt, Pass and Kick Competition, competed on a traveling soccer team, and was the quarterback of the Ocean Springs High Greyhounds. Funny and irreverent, Mike was very popular in high school and college. I introduced Mike to my sorority sister, Wendy, and they became college sweethearts.

They broke up after college and Wendy was about to marry someone else, but called off the wedding. I encouraged Mike to call her and reconnect. They did and they were about to get married.

Early one morning, I received an urgent call from my mom. Mike had been in a terrible car accident outside of Memphis. He was being airlifted to the Elvis Presley Trauma Center and it didn't look good. I leapt in my car and drove to Memphis from Atlanta to be with my family.

When I got to Memphis, I learned that Mike was in a deep coma. He had a pretty severe head injury. The doctors told us that "if" he made it, he'd have to relearn everything—how to talk, walk, and live. The doctors told us that he would never go back to normal, never have a full-time job, and would always need to be in someone else's care.

Mike was in a coma for over 18 days in the ICU in Memphis. My parents basically moved into his house in Southaven so they could be there every day. I traveled from Atlanta every weekend and my sister, Blake, was there as much as she could be during the week and on every weekend.

On the 19th day, Mike awoke from his coma. He started talking about football and his job at the bank. His speech was slurred and he still couldn't walk, but we had hope.

Mike was moved to rehab at HealthSouth, where he had an amazing rehabilitation team that included his lead therapist Megan and an occupational therapist. They set out to heal Mike. Mike was so incredibly determined to get back to normal and heal. He pushed his trainers to do more and train more, because he wanted to not only survive, but thrive.

Today the only symptom Mike shows is a slight drag on his right side when he walks, which is interesting because the head injury was on his left side and didn't impact his leg. Also, the scar from his tracheostomy tube is still visible.

Mike is the president of a bank in Ocean Springs. He and Wendy have two beautiful, successful daughters. Mike is involved in many boards and was named Rotarian of the Year and "Hometown Hero" in Ocean Springs.

In a beautiful twist of fate, my sister Blake worked for HealthSouth and heard someone at a conference speaking about "Miracle Mike" from 20 years ago. During the talk they highlighted the focused determination, hard work, and grit of Mike, who is a true success story in every aspect.

AHA MOMENT

As a partner on the leadership team and having reported to so many CEOs over the years, I've learned that alignment with the CEO is necessary. CEOs expect their marketing lead to help them grow their current business, grow into new segments, innovate, and become the heart of the organization. Seeking excellence is different from being a perfectionist. Excellence is teaching, coaching, showing up on time, being prepared, delivering on promises, partnering with peers, seeing things from their perspective, having a servant's heart, being kind, resilient, authentic, and openly expressing gratitude. Excellence also requires hitting the spell check (smile).

There are so many pressures on our time, whether it's our family, work, traffic, health, quality of life, burn out, or simply just not having fun. I've learned if I can't change the situation, I change the way it affects me. The choice is mine and mine alone. With the encouragement of my executive coach, Henna Inam, I graphed out how I was spending my time. I learned at the time, I didn't have much of a life outside of work.

One of my early methods, a dirty little secret to "success" at work, was working all weekend. Because I was in meetings all week, I'd use the weekends to build out PowerPoints, answer emails that needed a lot of attention, and tackle anything administrative that didn't require "face time." I didn't have a full life. Through lots of coaching and reflection, I learned that what you do, what you think and how you act *is* who you are. I didn't want my job to become the only meaningful aspect of my life.

PERSONAL TIME HAS TO BE SCHEDULED

My personal time became too important to just *let* things happen. I would have to make time for family, fitness, and fun, or it just wouldn't happen. I think about those tapes that reel in my brain and want to make sure they're playing happy tunes. The tune that plays in my head each morning is "Here Comes the Sun," by The Beatles. All this to say, enjoy life. It's the only one you have, the only one I have, and we are the CEOs of our own lives.

I was feeling overwhelmed and stressed when I was working all the time. I went to Canyon Ranch in Arizona with a group of friends to learn some healthy ways to reorient. According to the experts at Canyon Ranch, it takes 21 days to form a habit and only 72 hours to lose it. With exercise, the first five minutes is the hardest.

According to Michael J. Hewitt, Ph.D., research director of exercise science at Canyon Ranch, health can be visualized as a four-legged platform on which vitality and longevity rest. The four foundations on this platform are:

▸ Physical activity
▸ Optimal nutrition
▸ Stress management
▸ Sleep

EXERCISE IS THE FOUNTAIN OF YOUTH

It goes without saying that exercise, good nutrition, and movement trigger the brain and have huge benefits. If you are able to go to Canyon Ranch, go. It's an incredible gift you can give to yourself! It's a beautiful spot, with hiking, biking, medical coaches, seminars and delicious food. Here are some healthy hints for healthy habits that I took away from Canyon Ranch.

- Use a calendar, day planner, or computer to keep track of your exercise.
- Set an alarm to remind you to keep an appointment with yourself.
- Ask your kids to put a gold star on your calendar when you complete your goal for yourself.
- Put a big water bottle on your desk or in your car.
- Use notes to keep yourself focused.
- Freeze food in single portions.
- When you cook, double the recipe and save the rest.
- Delegate wherever you can.
- Make a roadmap of where you want to be in a month, six months.
- Listen to podcasts on subjects you need advice on.
- Shop online to save time.

PELOTON RELIGION

I have had a Peloton bike for three years and have become an addict. Their instructors are like preachers from the pulpit sharing good vibes and lessons they've learned. I feel like I always have a friend when I do a Peloton workout. The bike is awesome, but the app is even better for meditating, running, walking, and strength training.

The beautiful and talented Ally Love became my savior during the pandemic. She sprinkles the gospel through her Sunday "Feel Good Ride."

Ally Love said, "I go to the 9:30 service at Redeemer Downtown on 14th Street, and I love hearing the sermon. It grounds me, reminds me how great God has been to me, my family and friends, and I leave more knowledgeable. Timothy Keller, the founding pastor of Redeemer in Manhattan, is a well-known author, so I knew I wanted to check out his teaching when I came to New York. I found Redeemer and fell in love with the Bible-based teaching. That's a priority to me. We can all preach on feelings, but teaching on truth is what I live for, and learn from.

"Right after church, I walk to 23rd Street and teach a 12:45 class at Peloton. It's a live class that is broadcast to all bikes and app members. It's literally my 'Feel Good Ride'—the name of the class—as it allows me to bridge the gap of how great I feel from church and being on the bike, working out with thousands of riders at the same time, inspiring them through uplifting and encouraging language."

"I love Peloton because of its community. It's not only the leader in the hybrid of technology and fitness, but we are able to build social relationships that are magnified both on the bike, which uses a leaderboard that syncs with other riders, and off the bike, through real friendships across the country."

—ANDREW COTTO,

The New York Times, *March 8, 2019*

My favorite Ally Love quotes:

▸ "May we choose to be kind, not just nice. For our work on Earth is deeply rooted in true kindness."

▸ "We must be more thorough in our understanding than we are in our thoughts."

▸ "Stop talking about how short life is, and start living it."

▸ "There is a big difference between self-care and selfishness."

I also love Tunde Oyeneyin and recommend following her. If you are feeling sad, angry or discouraged, take the "Speak Out" ride with Tunde. She recorded it shortly after George Floyd's homicide and it is incredibly powerful and moving. She includes quotes about racism from fellow Peloton instructors that will hit you right in the heart. Commit to 30 minutes one day and take this class.

A few of my other favorite Peloton instructors are Robin Arzon, Emma Lovewell, Alex Toussaint, and Cody Rigsby. You don't even need the bike to use their amazing app that has so many workouts, including meditation, strength training, outdoor activities, running, sleep meditation, and many more.

I recently took Emma Lovewell's 45-minute live D.J. party class and through their brilliant app, was able download the music and continue to enjoy the playlists.

Robin Arzon composed a Facebook post that is too good not to share. She wrote, "A truly impassioned career is filled with meaningful work. One of the most common questions I get when it comes to this topic is how I knew when it was time to make a major change. One way to determine this is to 'zoom out' and assess how you feel at the end of your day. When you are in alignment, you feel really good about what you are doing (most of the time!)..."

Jeff Perkins is the Chief Executive Officer at ParkMobile and a friend in my posse. We love participating in the "Ride and Raise" events on Peloton. It's a way to donate to nonprofits while getting a good ride on the bike. His favorite quotes from Robin Arzon are, "We don't do basic" and "You can do anything, but you can't do everything."

OUTSOURCE EVERYTHING EXCEPT FITNESS, FAMILY, AND BEING PRESENT

Kayla Deuley Williams, a corporate wellness guru and friend, delegates everything she can that doesn't require her own personal touch. This includes, laundry, cleaning, and anything administrative. Carla Guy, a partner at Dagger Agency and mom of three, outsources everything beyond work and family. This includes shopping, having her car washed at work, and cleaning.

My exercise cheerleader is Karyn Froseth. Karyn and I work out two or three days a week. She's also my "chardonnay sister" and funny bestie. As I've been writing this book, Jeff Hilimire has been my accountability partner and cheerleader. Since he's "been there, done that" and is writing his fourth book, he's someone I've leaned on for advice and encouragement. While you think of how you are going to put your plan into action, think about someone you can count on to be your partner in achieving your goals in life.

LOVING YOURSELF

I have learned to determine what the most important things in my life are and started ignoring ones that I wasn't jazzed about. Once I started calendaring things, the trips with Lily to Disney World and to see the family in Ocean Springs happened! Owning my story and loving myself, and those around me, was the best, bravest, and boldest thing I've ever done.

I know I don't want to be on my deathbed wishing I had spent more time perfecting a PowerPoint deck or on a Zoom call. Country music singers never croon about creating a PowerPoint. Their songs are about love, family, and driving a truck.

Write yourself a love letter today.

Dear _____,

Have I told you lately how much I love you?
Though I've known you a long time, you still
amaze me. To me you are beautiful, especially
_____ and your _____.
I am especially proud of you when you
_____.

I love you,

Love letters and expressions like these to ourselves are like having tiny champagne bubbles in our brains, sparking off endorphins and good vibes to our being. Make time for self-care and self-love.

A GUIDE FOR "GOING FOR IT"!

Take the CliftonStrengths assessment. Write down your top five strengths.

1. _____
2. _____
3. _____
4. _____
5. _____

Find an accountability cheerleader to help on your journey.

JOJO'S GOGO

- [ ] *Use the planning time as "me time" and celebrate successes—big and small*
- [ ] *Establish reasons and rituals, scheduling in fun time with family and friends*
- [ ] *Dream about future goals and write them down*
- [ ] *Use my minutes and moments to create meaningful memories*
- [ ] *Find shows that make me laugh out loud*
- [ ] *Learn to play tennis!*
- [ ] *Celebrate this year at Canyon Ranch*

LIL' DITTY

Be the one who chose to go for it,
Have determination, grace and grit.
Do what you love and go for it,
With a good plan and strength not to quit.

6

Personality and Play— Glow with Authenticity

Always believe something good is going to happen.

Oprah said, "I believe the energy I put out is the energy I get back, always." I've lived by this proverb. She also said, "You don't become what you want, you become what you believe."

We are our actions, words, and thoughts—karma. There is a certain spirituality about how to show up. By consistently considering the following, we're more likely to live the lives we wish to lead:

▶ Our deepest experiences of meaning, values, identity, and purpose.

▸ Our sense of connection and relationships.

▸ Our awareness of forces within and beyond ourselves.

▸ Our belief in a higher order or being that transcends the created world.

Lisa Redstone, a former Canyon Ranch spiritual guidance provider, believes that complete well-being consists of balance between four dimensions:

1. **Physical:** Determining the right amount of exercise, nutrition, and balance in the body.

2. **Mental:** Determining the self-talk and attitudes I have. Asking what do I say to myself? Do I live in my head? Can I let go of that thinking?

3. **Emotional:** What do I honestly feel? Feelings are good—they just want to be felt.

4. **Spiritual:** What spiritual practices do I have? When do I feel connected? Is it prayer, nature, meditation, silence, silence, breath, awareness, intention?

GLOW STICK

Maintaining a spiritual practice can lead to clarity, health benefits, wisdom, balance, growth, and increased creativity. As I work to become a daily spiritual practitioner, I've noted that what helps me maintain a steady routine are a gratitude journal, regular exercise, random acts of kindness, and finding joy in the routine by dancing, singing, and laughing out loud. When you train your brain to see the good in most things, a notable increase in good vibes will begin to surround you. Positivity is a choice. It seems the biggest challenge in life is to be yourself in a world that is trying to make you like everyone else. Remind yourself of your truth and heed the words of Shakespeare's Polonius, "This above all; to thine own self be true..."

MEET DR. DAWN

Dr. Dawn Marie Kier is a former colleague from HoneyBaked who went on to get her PhD in Organizational Leadership. She is a coach and values expert whom I adore working with whenever I have the opportunity. She encourages constant inquiry, telling me to ask myself "How are you showing up? Are you the same at work as you are at home or at church?" She's led some soul-searching exercises with my teams at HoneyBaked and Interface. To know her is to know a bubbly, intelligent, intuitive lady who leads her life with purpose, values, vision, and grace.

Dawn uses a system called "The Values Cards" during a powerful exercise she leads. Every person in the room is given a pack of value cards. These value cards are based on the Theory of Basic Human Values, which was pioneered by social psychologist Shalom H. Schwartz. You can find them on Amazon. From the 83 values card choices, you sort them into piles. The categories are:

- ▸ Very Important to Me
- ▸ Important to Me
- ▸ Not Important to Me
- ▸ Somewhat Important to Me
- ▸ Most Important to Me

During this timed exercise, the participants are asked to rank their personal values using this tool. It's an amazingly simple, but effective, way to discover the personal values that may hide themselves behind your day-to-day routine. I recall one teammate changing her career because of what she learned about herself.

BE WHO YOU ARE, ALWAYS

My dad is exactly the same person whether at work, fishing, at church, or volunteering. He can be shockingly funny by telling off-color jokes, and also generous, kind, and welcoming to all. He still hosts a fish fry for all his colleagues at Northrop Grumman, where he ultimately retired. His posse shows up because they know they'll enjoy the freshest red fish caught by Mike, snack on fried pickles, linger, laugh in the warm hug that he creates, and listen to his hilarious jokes and funny stories.

My mentor, Randy Hain, founder and president of Serviam Partners, is a lot like my dad. He loves his family and is incredibly gentle and kind. In his book, Randy writes that these are the essential components to authenticity in the business setting:

- ▸ Pay It Forward.
- ▸ Be Candid.
- ▸ Invite Transparency with Transparency.
- ▸ Earn Trust.
- ▸ Bring Consistency and Dependability.
- ▸ Live with Insatiable Curiosity.
- ▸ Listen Actively.
- ▸ Connect With Affinity.
- ▸ Behave with Mutual Respect and Civility.

The "five-minute favor" is something I have discovered from one of my favorite books, *Give and Take,* by Adam Grant. It's fun to "pay it forward" and make introductions to like-minded people, to write LinkedIn references without being asked, and to do kind things for others. Randy Hain has inspired me to do so through his numerous acts of random kindness.

> *"To be yourself in a world that is constantly trying to make you something else is the greatest accomplishment."*
> – RALPH WALDO EMERSON

BE BRAVE, BE BOLD, BE A HONEYDRAGON

Russ Klein, former CMO at Arby's and former CEO at the American Marketing Association, gave our marketing team copies of Brené Brown's *Daring Greatly* when I was there over eight years ago. Since reading her book, I've become a devotee.

A few of my favorite Brené Brown sayings:

▸ "You either walk inside your story and own it, or you stand outside your story and hustle for your worthiness."

When I was working so hard and didn't have a life, I didn't know my neighbors. I'd try to zip into my house and dodge them after a long day of work. One of the joys of breaking away from the "work all the time" mentality is now I work hard to be personable and get to know my neighbors. I try to know their names, go on walks with them, invite them over and vice versa, and just have fun.

When we lived on Oakdale Road in Atlanta, Mark and I decided to form a neighborhood alliance after our car was broken into. We collected the names of our neighbors and threw a meet and greet. From that meet and greet, we discovered that many of the neighbors had never met and some of the elderly neighbors on the street hadn't seen each other in over 30 years. When we moved from friendly Pasadena, we wondered why no one had ever greeted us. What we discovered from getting out and talking to our neighbors on Oakdale is that it's a backyard neighborhood— the lots are huge.

That said, everyone on the street wanted a reason to get together, but there wasn't an organizer or a catalyst to do so. We decided to be the spark and reason. From that little meet and greet to now, we have some of our best friends and neighbors on Oakdale Road in Atlanta. That group is called the WOOs (Women of Oakdale) and the men are dubbed as the MOOs (Men of Oakdale).

From these friendships, we were able to raise money to erect street lights on the dark street, add a bench, and maintain a small park in Emory Village. We have had countless happy hours and welcoming parties for new neighbors. We've formed and maintained friendships with some of our widowed elderly neighbors and Mark saved one of their lives. But I digress...

HONEYDRAGON

The term HoneyDragon came out of HoneyBaked's relationship with Dragon Army, a web design and technology agency led by Jeff Hilimire. A collaboration with the collective Dragon Army team and the HoneyBaked Marketing and Information Team sparked into a team name called the HoneyDragons. What I loved about this partnership was that it was based on honesty, transparency, and trust, while fiercely meeting our goals to modernize our digital presence at HoneyBaked. When I need to be kind, but tough, I put the HoneyDragon moniker in my brain.

BE YOURSELF, ALWAYS

Authenticity and connections are so powerful. As a matter of fact, and as I am writing this, it occurred to me how authenticity can play into all areas. At HoneyBaked, our vision is to be authentic in all we do.

There's a double meaning in authenticity for HoneyBaked. First, The Honey Baked Ham Company is the original, the gold standard, and there is no substitute. On the personal level, authenticity is about the way HoneyBaked's associates show up by leveraging our genuineness, realness, being humble, and serving others. Authenticity is true to the brand and has been a rallying statement for all of our communications, including advertising, web copy, and training in our store and customer service environments. Our internal moniker is the #hamfam and one of our values is to "do what we love, love what we do."

GUIDE FOR AUTHENTICITY

1. What am I grateful for today?

_____

_____

_____

_____

_____

_____

_____

2. What is a random act of kindness or five-minute favor for today?

_____

_____

_____

_____

_____

_____

_____

3. Meet a new neighbor or call an old friend.

4. Schedule lunch or Zoom with a colleague.

JOJO'S GOGO

- [ ] Host a block party in the spring for the neighbors with Mark
- [ ] Meditate and pray
- [ ] Moderate diet by eating healthier in the new year

LIL' DITTY

Be who you are, and you will go far,
Be kind, authentic, always raising the bar.
Be authentic, be your own North Star.
Have a HoneyDragon spirit and be who you are.

7

Powerful Pursuit

Do epic shit.

Being poised, calm, and collected takes a lot of practice. I used to be perpetually late to anything and everything. In 2015, I made a goal and a commitment to be on time for things. What a difference that has made. I have less stress, less anxiety, and get to enjoy whatever it is I've committed to on the calendar. For this year, I have a goal to arrive early to appointments. With the exception of dinner parties where it's rude to be early, I am attempting to cultivate a habit of showing up early. While waiting, I can listen to NPR, check texts, or go for a quick walk.

I am also working on public speaking and striving to be really good at it. Most of us struggle with public speaking anxiety. Several years ago, I saw one of my most talented teammates at

Arby's almost pass out when he was asked to deliver a speech to a small audience on the marketing team. It was a fight-or-flight moment for him and was very hard to watch this smart, talented marketer struggle in this situation.

Some of my favorite quotes on public speaking are:

- ▸ "Grasp the subject, the words will follow." –*Cato the Elder*

- ▸ "Be sincere, be brief, be seated." –*Franklin D. Roosevelt*

- ▸ "It usually takes more than three weeks to prepare a good impromptu speech." –*Mark Twain*

- ▸ "Speech is power: speech is to persuade, to convert, to compel." –*Ralph Waldo Emerson*

- ▸ "Knowledge speaks, but wisdom listens." –*Jimi Hendrix*

Almost 75 percent of the population is afraid to speak in public. Public speaking used to terrify me. Jerry Seinfeld said, "According to most studies, people's number one fear is public speaking. Number two is death. Death is number two. Does that sound right? This means to the average person, if you go to a funeral, you're better off in the casket than delivering the eulogy."

Despite being one of the best-selling recording artists of all time, Barbra Streisand has crippling stage fright. While she has overcome her anxiety, she doesn't perform anymore because she doesn't enjoy it and worries she will let down her crowd.

It helped to know I was not alone in my public speaking phobia. I bombed a speech in my early 20s trying to get buy-in on marketing programs to some of our key franchisees. Thankfully, I had a very kind boss who had my back and encouraged me to join a Dale Carnegie class. It was a very humbling, yet extraordinary gift, to be able to have that training. Sometimes I go back and read Dale Carnegie's book, *How to Win Friends & Influence People*, as the passages and principles are timeless.

BE UNFLAPPABLE

Prepare for meetings and know what the agenda will be. Get to the meeting early and figure out where you want to sit and who you want to sit by. Speak up, as appropriate, and have a point of view on the subject. That said, Katie Kirkpatrick, CEO of the Metro Atlanta Chamber of Commerce, suggests, "Let five people speak before you speak again."

Volunteer to take on action steps. Also, if someone is not capturing the next steps in a meeting, do so, and send out the outcome of the meeting in meeting notes.

THE 6 KEY STEPS TO A GREAT MEETING

- ▸ Consider your desired outcome.
- ▸ Create an agenda.
- ▸ Identify and invite key participants.
- ▸ Present the issues and stay focused on the goal.
- ▸ Wrap up the meeting.
- ▸ Send out the meeting notes and next steps.

SPEAK OUT

Starting out in business can be intimidating. Speaking with confidence when persuading franchisees or cross-functional team members requires skill. Think through your tone when speaking and make statements instead of asking questions.

Early in my career, my boss, Marty Fagan, told me I was speaking too softly and that our older franchisees couldn't hear me. He mentioned that I should not phrase my comments as questions, but as emphatic statements to ensure the programs we were selling into our franchise teams were presented with confidence and assurance.

For example:

DO'S	DON'TS
We will win!	Will we win?
Let's do this!	Let's do this?

Think through your voice pitch also. Make sure it's clear, void of "ums" and pauses. The pitch should be low, not high, and bold, not meek.

In the early days of my career, becoming a great public speaker was a goal, and it still is. Through lots of coaching, trial and error, practice, sweat, and tears, I now do quite a bit of public speaking. Do I get nervous? Hell yeah, but have I overcome my fears? Yes, for sure, and I am now confident that when I am asked to speak, I'll be able to deliver a compelling message if I practice and prepare for the event and tailor the message to the audience.

Another tip for overcoming public speaking is to join Toastmasters. I did this when Mark and I lived in Pasadena and felt very vulnerable about it. However, and in doing so, not only did I learn some good tips in a very safe environment, I also made some new friends in a new city. One of the reasons I also wanted to become an adjunct marketing professor is so that I could practice getting in front of crowds.

GIVE 'EM SOMETHING TO TALK ABOUT

Writing, good storytelling, and practice, practice, practice is the key to delivering a good speech. That, and speaking on a subject that you are an expert on. Serving on panels is also a great way to get public speaking experience. And, an added benefit is that I've gotten to meet some fascinating folks on panels —some who have become great friends.

I've also been taking risks with some of my presentations including having a vocalist come alongside and beatbox the message I was giving to the Interface sales team. We received a standing ovation from the "hard to please" sales leaders. The next year, at the Interface sales meeting, I threaded Muhammad Ali quotes, lyrics, and videos with some of my favorite Beatles songs to create and deliver a rap poem.

Storytelling is an art. Crafting a story arc—which is a literary term— is the chronological construction of a story and has highs and lows, ups and downs, and then up again. It's also damn fun for the audience to hear a riveting story.

Recognizing that with any speech or presentation, I respect that my role is to provide insights and entertain the audience. I know the audience is rooting for my success and also know that I have exactly three seconds for the audience to connect with me. From Jane Pierotti and the StoryMap workshop at the Duarte Academy, I learned the opening has to be captivating to capture the crowd, the middle of the speech can be content, and the end has to be killer!

The graph below is from Nancy Duarte's TED talk:

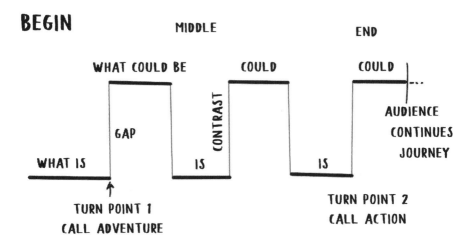

To calm my nerves before a speech, I get there early, work with the tech team, and laugh with them as I am getting microphoned up. I imagine the best possible scenario, as well as make eye contact and smile with the audience. I had a speech coach help me with some of the more important speeches I've given. I'd practiced, practiced, practiced, and prepped.

Jane's public speaking tips are:

▸ Wear a great outfit.

▸ Own the stage. Walk on strong, smiling, and confident.

▸ Have a story you want to tell—open the speech with the story.

▸ Use the story to give examples of the messages you want to communicate.

▸ Use props and big gestures on stage.

- ▸ Move away from the podium and walk the stage.

- ▸ Use music, visuals, or whatever it takes to seduce the audience.

- ▸ Keep Powerpoint to a minimum and keep it simple. Have them focus on you.

- ▸ Have a powerful close so that the crowd remembers what you said.

Jeff Perkins, CEO at Park Mobile, shared this quote I love from Bruce Springsteen, "Getting an audience is hard. Sustaining an audience is hard. It demands a consistency of thought, of purpose, and of action for a long period of time."

KNOW HOW TO READ A ROOM

Reading the room is an important part of a presentation. The best way to read a room is to pay close attention to people—and not just what they're saying. Do a scan of the room and note, are people smiling, or are they on their phones, or are they talking to others? Who's standing, who's sitting, and how much space is between people? Next, try to pick up on their expressions—do they look happy or tense?

Control how much you are talking, and watch and observe. Whether you're in a room with a large group of people, a small group, or you're speaking with a colleague one-on-one, really actively listen to what the other person is saying. Be present, acknowledge what the other is saying, make eye contact, and lean into the conversation.

Let the other person know that you are in the moment and the conversation together.

Once you've observed the energy in the room, try to get a read on how you think it's going. Check in with a trusted colleague and get a gut check. If you feel the room getting heated, use humor to shift the tone and lighten the situation.

DO'S	DON'TS
Take a moment to feel the energy in the room.	Get distracted—take the moment to be present and engaged. Make eye contact.
Look at people's expressions. Are they smiling? Looking tense?	Be shy. Walk the room and engage. Ask others how they are doing.
Look for the people who are smiling and engaged. Leverage them as role models.	Go down with any negativity. Stay positive and keep the energy positive.

COMMUNICATORS EXTRAORDINAIRE

▸ Kat Cole is probably the best communicator I've ever been around. Authentic and totally relaxed in her own skin, she exudes a likability and confidence to everyone who is lucky enough to be in her sphere.

▶ Nancy Duarte is as genuine as they come. She and I became friends after we worked on a project at Interface. I did attend one of Duarte's storytelling workshops in Palo Alto and use her methodology when crafting a big presentation. We also had a colleague of hers give a workshop for the global marketing team at Interface. And if you have never read any of Nancy Duarte's books like *The Art and Science of Creating Great Presentations* or *Resonate: Present Visual Stories that Transform Audiences,* go do it now. Nancy also has one of my favorite TED talks.

▶ Moreover, a former colleague at Interface, George Bandy, is someone who has "it." George is an expert in sustainability and is a global connector. He is always dressed in a dapper suit and is never seen without a big, beautiful smile and radiant positivity.

▶ Jeff Hilimire has a sincere, humble genuineness to him that connects with the audience.

▶ Kate Atwood is an amazing storyteller and uses emotion and real examples to captivate her viewers in her presentations.

▶ No one commanded an audience like Martin Luther King, Jr. I've studied Martin Luther King Jr.'s powerful messages and stories about creating a movement. He's my hero.

▶ Douwe Bergsma, Chief Marketing Officer at Piedmont Healthcare and formerly at Georgia Pacific, uses storytelling as a key differentiator with his messaging and marketing.

A BRAND YOU CAN TRUST

I have struggled with the "Brand You" and "Become a Personal Brand" mantras. For some reason, they don't feel genuine to me. However, great brands are brands that make a promise and deliver on that promise over and over and over. We trust strong brands.

Think about your favorite brands.

- ▸ My favorite brands are:
- ▸ Why?

My favorite brands are Apple, Volvo, Delta Air Lines, Peloton, and LaCroix. The reason is that they are a part of my daily life, they are trustworthy and make things a little bit better for me. So, given that reasoning, I like to think about ways that I can be a person someone trusts.

Mike Popowski, CEO of Dagger, says that "Smart brands act like media companies pushing out original content." His agency partnered with us when I was at Interface. They served alongside our global team to give us a global, digital presence. The Dagger team dove in and understood the nuances of communicating around the world and were invaluable partners as we moved from a highly localized digital presence to communicating as a strong, singular design brand. Dagger also publishes its own content through the site @butter.atl, which has become the Atlanta culture channel and produces cultural events.

Create your elevator pitch. This should be no more than 30 to 60 seconds long. These are five basic elements you need to include:

- ▸ **Profession:** State your personal identity in the present tense. "I am a marketing executive."

- **Expertise:** State your competencies or expertise. "With an expertise in brand transformation, innovation, and team leadership."

- **Types of Organizations:** Provide a summary of the organizations you have worked for. "For iconic consumer and business-to-business brands, including The Honey Baked Ham Company, Arby's, and Interface."

- **Unique Strengths:** Identify the areas that make you uniquely qualified. "My strengths include visioning, strategic planning, innovation around product development and digital transformation. I am a brand and turnaround expert."

Here is a good template to use:

I am a _____ with expertise in _____, _____ and _____. I have worked with _____ in the _____ industry. My strengths include _____, _____ and _____. I am a _____ and _____ expert.

Here's mine:

"I am a marketing executive with expertise in brand transformation, innovation and team leadership. I have worked with iconic consumer and B2B brands, including The Honey Baked Ham Company, Arby's, and Interface. My strengths include visioning, strategic planning, and innovation. I am a brand transformation and turnaround expert."

From there, develop your bio with an awesome photo. A bio is extremely useful and can be used when making introductions, getting on boards, and on your LinkedIn profile. Here's an example of mine.

A marketing and brand transformation expert, Jo Ann has a track record of delivering robust financial results and award-winning marketing programs that build sales and profitability for iconic brands in the B2B and B2C space. Jo Ann formerly served as Chief Marketing Officer for The Honey Baked Ham Company.

As Chief Marketing Officer for Interface, Inc., she globalized the marketing team and brought forth a highly effective, integrated marketing approach resulting in five consecutive quarters of record-breaking financial growth. Prior to Interface, she served as Vice President of Brand Marketing and Public Relations at Arby's Restaurant Group resulting in a brand turnaround and 13 quarters of same-store sales growth. Prior to Arby's, she spent 16 years at HoneyBaked, where she served as Vice President of Marketing and later as Chief Marketing Officer. She also has owned her own marketing firm, The Marketing Department.

Jo Ann has an MBA in International Business from Mercer University in Atlanta and bachelor's degree in communication from Mississippi State University. She is a passionate community volunteer and served as Vice Chair of the Arby's Foundation, whose mission is to end childhood hunger. Her work has been lauded by industry and community groups including the National Diversity Council's

Most Powerful and Influential Women, the prestigious Best Neighbor Award from the National Restaurant Association, two AMY Awards from the American Marketing Association, a Phoenix Award for community volunteerism, and an Effie Award for advertising effectiveness. She recently received a Lifetime Achievement Award from the American Marketing Association and received the President's Award from the CMO Club.

Jo Ann was the president of the 1,000-member Atlanta chapter of the AMA in 2018. She is currently a Vice Chair of the board for the Atlanta Convention and Visitors Bureau. She is a graduate of the 2012 Leadership Atlanta class.

Jo Ann and her husband Mark live in Druid Hills with their daughter, Lily. They love to walk with their French Bulldog, Gatsby.

BECOME A SOCIAL BUTTERFLY

I love social media and am one of the few people who also enjoys getting personalized ads served up to me based on my likes and dislikes.

Consider your digital presence…think about your posts, your tone, your photos. When applying for a job, recruiters look at your digital footprint for fit.

From a business perspective, LinkedIn is the main tool. It's the main tool that recruiters use when sourcing candidates. Think about this when setting up your LinkedIn profile.

▸ Have a professional photo on your profile.

- ▶ Have a background image that expresses who you are.

- ▶ Leverage key words (that recruiters will search when sourcing candidates) when creating your experience.

- ▶ Use your bio (from above) in the "About" section.

- ▶ Find projects that you are proud of and highlight them in the "Featured" section. This could be video projects you've worked on, articles you are featured in, or podcasts where you've contributed.

- ▶ Build out your experience and showcase measurable results.

- ▶ Include all education and showcase organizations you are involved with.

- ▶ Build out the volunteering section.

- ▶ Get recommendations. I have hired candidates based on their recommendations. Annie Carlini at Interface is someone we hired to be on the brand team based on the number of recommendations she had and the profusive way they were written by people in her circle.

- ▶ Showcase your accomplishments including honors and awards, being mentioned in publications, and courses you have taken. Build up your number of followers—this will help you get to the top of the list with recruiters.

- ▶ Be active on LinkedIn.

Facebook helps me stay connected with friends and family. When I was traveling internationally for Interface, I made friends around the globe. Facebook has been a fun way to keep in touch and see what family, friends, and colleagues are up to. Instagram is a quick and easy way to see beautiful postings and inspirational quotes. I am on Twitter and follow, but am not active on the platform.

STRUT YOUR STUFF

Communication is king, but in all areas of life, I do believe you can have anything you want in life if you dress for it. Dressing has a mood-altering effect and I use clothes to express myself. I love matching eclectic pieces together and making the outfit interesting. While I am writing this, we are in the middle of the pandemic, and are working from home. However, there are still ways to highlight style while on Zoom. Stylist Rachel Zoe said, "Style is a way to say who you are without having to speak." Dressing well is a creative expression.

Clothes can change my vibe and if I am feeling like:

▸ A badass, it's a furry shirt, jeans, cowboy boots, and dangly, chandelier rhinestone earrings.

▸ A board member, it's a Manolo strappy stiletto, a Theory dress, and earrings that Mark gave me for a big birthday.

▸ An athlete, it's Lululemon leggings, a shirt with a funny saying, On Cloud tennis shoes, and old school pom-pom socks.

▸ A dinner out with my husband and friends, it's a Veronica Beard Dickey jacket, jeans, boots, and earrings from Mark.

▸ A meeting at work, it's a Vince leather jacket, white jeans, Frye boots, and heart earrings from the American Marketing Association.

- A speech for the Brand Innovators, it's a Diane von Furstenberg dress, and Christian Louboutin shoes/heels.

- A dinner with the Leadership Atlanta posse, it's a bright red shirt from Haute Hippie, Current/Elliott skinny black jeans, suede Frye boots, hair up in a bun, and fun earrings.

- A neighborhood backyard concert, it's a black shirt, a fun scarf, a denim jacket, white pants, and metallic Golden Goose shoes.

WHEN BAD FASHION HURTS

When I started working in the corporate environment in the 80s, there was a book for women called *Dress for Success*. Written by a man, he encouraged women to dress like their male counterparts in gray or navy blue pinstripes, jackets with shoulder pads, and sport uncomfortable nude panty hose and high heel pumps. Can you imagine the blisters and the amount of finger nail polish we used to stop the panty hose runs?

Without a guidebook and very few women role models, it was a very unfortunate time for businesswomen and fashion. Sadly, during this time, for many women, this book was our bible for dressing and rising up the ranks. I am so happy the next generation of awesome women will not have to endure this.

To be fair, the men during the 80s, 90s, and 2000s were encouraged to wear starched shirts, flashy ties, and uncomfortable shoes, as well. It's amazing to see how the dress code has changed at work over the decades.

STYLE IS SAYING WHO YOU ARE WITHOUT HAVING TO SPEAK

When I was the head of communications at Arby's, I coached the senior executives on their speeches and all communications. It was a role where I had to exude confidence and professionalism. A day could involve writing a speech, communicating with the powerful franchise organization, working with the private equity group, or, most often, dealing with a crisis. I loved working for Arby's and walked into the building knowing that something good was going to happen every day.

A role on the communications team was highly sought after and anyone who joined the team would be coached by me on the importance of dressing well and professionally since they would be working with and consulting the most senior leaders in the organization. I recruited Anna Webb, one of our up-and-coming brand managers, to serve as a director on the communications team. During the interview process we talked about how important wardrobe would be and dressing the part. Anna, a style icon in her own right, completely agreed and supplemented her already cool style with smart jackets and sophisticated suits.

The key is that dressing well doesn't need to break the bank, either. It could be a cute jacket from J. Crew or Nordstrom's. How one dresses gives people cues, impressions, and shapes their opinions about the person in the role.

BEST-DRESSED

Dress like a fashion boss! My best-dressed list includes:

- Kat Cole can often be seen in a black turtleneck, black pants and boots—Kat keeps it simple and beautiful.

- Hala Moddelmog, one of my early mentors, has a gorgeous collection of suits, heels, and a very creative wardrobe. She also has good posture and radiates when she walks into a room.

- John Wells, former president of Interface, could often be seen in a navy blue pinstripe shirt and preppy white pants—all while high-fiving and flashing a big smile.

- Charley Knight, former VP of hospitality at Interface, wore the brand color for the Interface segment he represented, pink, so that he would stand out with his customers.

- David Gerson, wears a red poppy flower pin on his jacket lapel while gregariously meeting people in the room.

- The gentlemen at Roark Capital, a private equity group in Atlanta, love wearing purple ties.

- Julie Bowerman, Chief Marketing and Ecommerce Officer at Kellogg's, can be seen in velvet pants and a chic leather jacket or white Theory dress with sleek shoes.

- For Jeff Hilimire, CEO of Dragon Army, it's a cool T-shirt, jeans, and tennis shoes.

- Wendy Clark, global CEO of Dentsu International, wears a lot of David Yurman bracelets, a branded T-shirt, a great jacket, and a gorgeous smile.

- Joe Koufman, founder and CEO of Setup Marketing, wears an ear-to-ear smile that makes him a fashion icon.

▸ Lisa Lilienthal, Principal—Purpose Practice at Dialogue Marketing and Interface's long-standing PR consultant, has glowing blonde hair, beautiful blouses and scarves, and a positive approachability aura around her.

▸ My husband, Mark, is a big fan of Brooks Brothers, Peter Millar, and Frye or Cole Hahn shoes.

HANDWRITTEN NOTES AND KIND CONFETTI

Use beautiful stationery to send handwritten notes as a surprise and delight. Handwritten notes are a way to show gratitude and are a standout in a digital world. They are such a nice touch and are always valued. I keep handwritten notes sent by others in a treasured burlap bag. Every once in a while, I'll pull them out and read them. They bring a smile every time I do.

Your own fun style, a smile, and a great attitude are confidence building. For me, fashion and style are about whatever I am in the mood for that day, depending on the situation. That said, I know that when I wear a big, broad smile and throw kindness around like confetti, I am always in style.

GUIDE FOR BEING POWERFUL!

1. When is the next time I have to give a presentation?

_____

_____

_____

_____

_____

2. Am I ready for it? How will I prepare?

_____

_____

_____

_____

_____

3. What am I going to wear?

_____

_____

_____

_____

_____

4. Describe the best possible outcome.

_____

_____

_____

_____

_____

_____

_____

JOJO'S GOGO

☐ *Purge my closet of things I won't wear anymore and donate to Covenant House*

☐ *Show up early for all appointments—even on Zoom*

☐ *Have pizzazz, be well-dressed, and smile a lot for Zoom calls*

LIL' DITTY

It's OK to fake it till you make it,
When you are on the road to make a big hit.
Commit and go up and get it.
Goals are best when you make a run for it.

8

Perspiration and Innovation

Be brilliant.

Every one of us has a great capacity for brilliance. That's my humble opinion from over 30 years of working in marketing. Our brilliance translates to the products and services we sell, the people we serve, the stories we tell, and the experiences we create for our customers. It is true in any industry—transportation, consumer goods, services or nonprofit. It is also true for the different divisions in business—sales, marketing, human resources, legal, finance, supply chain, frontline employee, or freelancer/contractor.

But that brilliance is a moving target. Consumer demand changes. Innovation, globalization, consolidation, increased transparency into our work, and a never-ending need for ingenuity is the reality.

BRILLIANCE AMONG US

Examples of market shifts and disruptions all over the world:

▶ Airbnb has become the largest hotel chain—without a single real estate investment.

▶ Interface reduced its carbon footprint and offers carbon-neutral flooring products to the world.

▶ Netflix and other streaming services have reconfigured the entertainment industry.

▶ Uber has become the largest transportation company—without owning any vehicles.

▶ Amazon is shaking up the delivery space, redefining convenience, and modernizing grocery shopping.

▶ Instacart has reimagined how we shop for groceries.

Transformation is all around us. There has never been a more exciting time to be in business, but the rule books of yesteryear are no longer relevant. Think about how the office environment was before the pandemic. Going into the office from 9 to 5, Monday through Friday, is most likely a thing of the past. Videoconferencing has enabled us to be more productive while working remotely.

Design, creativity, and innovation are often built on hope, optimism and inspiration. And don't we all want to stand out from the crowd, stand up for doing good in the world, doing good work, and doing something epic? Don't we all want to increase our capacity for brilliance? Do I hear an amen?

MEET DAVE SUTTON

All of this leads me to Dave Sutton. Dave Sutton is someone who is at the top of my posse. Dave is the founder of TopRight, an innovative strategic consultancy in Atlanta. TopRight has a number of blue-chip clients and is always on the cutting edge of innovation, marketing, and technology.

Dave has written three books on marketing transformation. I wrote the foreword to Dave's book *Marketing Interrupted* and used some of the disruption examples listed above. I had the great pleasure of working with Dave and TopRight as their chief marketing officer and learned so many things from him and his team. Dave is always a snappy dresser and can always be seen with a bright smile.

Dave's favorite quote from Malcolm Gladwell is, "Transformation isn't about improving. It's about rethinking." His favorite piece of advice from his mom is, "You can't control other people's lives, but you can control your reaction to them."

Dave shared these top favorite marketing quotes and they are too good not to share with you:

▸ "A brand is no longer what we tell the consumer it is. It is what consumers tell each other it is." —*Scott Cook*

▸ "Good marketing makes the company look smart. Great marketing makes the customer feel smart." —*Joe Chernov*

- "If you are an artist, learn science. If you are a scientist, cultivate art." —*Karin Timpone*

- "Marketing is no longer about the stuff that you make, but about the stories you tell." —*Seth Godin*

- "Simplicity is the keynote of all true elegance."—*Coco Chanel*

- "The aim of marketing is to know and understand the customer so well the product or service fits him and sells itself...The aim of marketing is to make selling superfluous." —*Peter Drucker*

- "The stories that spread today empower us and give us belief in our own heroic potential." —*Jonah Sachs*

- "Ask yourself how you can deliver more value to your customers, not get more money from them." —*David Salyers*

- "Good marketers tell brand stories; great marketers tell them with purpose." —*Dave Sutton*

- "Make the customer the hero of your story."—*Ann Handley*

- "Speak to your audience in their language about what's in their heart." —*Jonathan Lister*

- "People don't buy what you do, they buy why you do it." —*Simon Sinek*

- " 'Youtility' is marketing so useful that people will pay for it." —*Jay Baer*

- "It's kind of fun to do the impossible." —*Walt Disney*

- "A year from now, you'll wish you had started today." —*Karen Lamb*

INNOVATION AT WORK

In all of my roles, I have had to be on the front end of innovation and transformation. It's not for the weak of heart when you are leading change. During my second time at HoneyBaked, I was asked to transform the brand look, our store design, and our menu. Innovation is not just about uncovering the next big idea—it's also about having a stick-to-itiveness approach to executing the ideas, changing the operation, and communicating in a new way.

When I returned back to HoneyBaked, one of the first key projects I had was to update our trademarks. Working with one of the best branding design firms in the world, Hornall Anderson, we set forth on a brand and design overhaul. Partnering with our CEO, our trademark attorneys, our franchisees, and operations partners, we were able to give a fun, youthful look to an iconic brand. The results were that our loyal customers loved it, but it also attracted a younger demographic who liked the retro look.

Because the brand look was so fresh, we created a branded clothing line, including shirts, jackets, skateboards, Vans shoes, and bikes. The new clothing line was a hit with our internal team and changed the way we dressed at HoneyBaked. A new, casual vibe was seen at the office and with our field team.

The HoneyBaked team took this great new branded look and updated our store design. Working with Callison, an architecture firm out of Seattle, we designed our store of the future in Alpharetta, Georgia. From there, we went on to innovate new products with the help of Barb Stuckey, and her team at Mattson out of San Francisco, California. Capitalizing on consumer trends of cleaner labels, easy-to-prepare meals, and comfort foods, we developed and launched a new line of delicious side dishes enabling us to innovate on our meal solutions and bundling.

WHAT TO DO WHEN YOU'RE GIVEN A BIG HAIRY PROJECT AND YOU'RE NOT SURE WHAT TO DO

I've been given some crazy assignments along the way. Some have involved government officials, law enforcement, and bleach (that is a long story). When confronted with something new and feeling that panicky, "what do I do" moment, here is what I do:

▸ Take some breaths. Not one breath, but four, and breathe from the belly.

▸ Count backwards from 10.

▸ Write down what I need to do and then break it down. Remember the saying, "How do you eat an elephant? One bite at a time!"

▸ If it's not a crisis and I have time to reflect, I'll go for a walk and meditate on the assignment.

▸ If it's out of my wheelhouse, I'll call some of the experts I know and pick their brains.

▸ I seek the advice of my teammates or people I have worked with in the past.

▸ When I start worrying, I start praying. I turn it over to a higher power.

- ▸ I'll keep working on the assignment until it's completed, not letting critics or negativity get me sidetracked. I show up, take the knocks, and am the honey badger of getting something over the line.

- ▸ I'll ask someone in my posse to meet for a glass of wine. Someone who is not involved who can give clarity, provide humor, and help me think the problem through.

- ▸ I go to the High Museum or Atlanta Botanical Gardens to seek beauty and inspiration.

GUIDE FOR INNOVATION

1. What is broken that needs to be fixed?

_____

_____

_____

_____

_____

2. What can I do to help solve the problem?

_____

_____

_____

_____

_____

3. Whose help do I need?

_____

_____

_____

_____

_____

JOJO'S GOGO

- ☐ *Finish this book*
- ☐ *Finalize innovation calendar personally and professionally for the year*
- ☐ *Design bucket list*

LIL' DITTY

Innovation can be exhilarating,
Motivation and big thinking are part of creating,
Have the courage to be the inspiration.
Do epic shit and take a vacation.

9

Positivity: Be a Positive Light in the World

Be the light, be the spark.

I wish I could have met the late, great Ray Anderson, the founder and first CEO of Interface, Inc. Some of his most cherished quotes are:

▸ "Brighten the corner where you are."

▸ "There is no more strategic issue for a company, or any organization, than its ultimate purpose. For those who think business exists to make a profit, I suggest they think again. Business makes a profit to exist. Surely, it must exist for some higher, nobler purpose than that."

▸ "We have a choice to make during our brief visit to this beautiful blue and green planet: to hurt it or to help it."

Powerful words from the business leader of a $1 billion organization whose product was not environmentally friendly, but ultimately became so because of his vision. Ray and his "Dream Team" pioneered a new, revolutionary way of thinking about business and our planet. Ray has an amazing TED Talk and it's awe-inspiring.

LIGHTNING IN A BOTTLE

Leadership is about being positive in negative situations. Leadership in a crisis is about being quiet when everyone else is being loud and being loud when everyone is quiet.

Leadership Atlanta has changed me in so many ways—whether it was better understanding race relations or how I, a white woman with privilege, can act. My paradigm shifted in so many positive ways. I have gone into deep learning about how I can help bring a point of view and have courageous conversations. For me, it's been about listening, reading, studying, and using my positive voice for good. It's about being brave and challenging the status quo. It's about interrupting when I see biases at every opportunity. Ever the optimist, I do believe we are at a tipping point for real change when it comes to social justice and I will continue to use my voice to speak out.

After the brutal killing of George Floyd and the subsequent protests and predominantly peaceful demonstrations in Atlanta, our Leadership Atlanta class convened for an impactful series of Zoom calls so that our teammates could connect and rally. The calls were raw, emotional, tense, extremely honest, and compelling. I read *White Fragility, A Raisin in the Sun, Becoming, How to Be an Antiracist* and devoured many other books and webinars that included or intricately explored racial injustice.

The late John Lewis was our district's congressman and I have studied his amazing work. It's one of the reasons I love Atlanta and am so proud to live here. It's not lost on me that Martin Luther King, Jr.'s home and church are only a few miles away from where we live. I am writing this passage on MLK Day and these are a few of my favorite quotes from him:

▶ "Darkness cannot drive out darkness, only light can do that. Hate cannot drive out hate, only love can do that."

▶ "The time is always right to do what is right."

▶ "In the end, we will remember not the words of our enemies, but the silence of our friends."

▶ "Our lives begin to end the day we become silent about things that matter."

Stacey Abrams, a Leadership Atlanta alum, is someone I admire greatly. Stacey is a *New York Times* bestselling author, an entrepreneur, a nonprofit CEO, has served our district in the Georgia House of Representatives, and has been at the forefront of Fair Fight—a movement to ensure every American has the right to vote in our election system. Stacey, like me, is from the Mississippi gulf coast and now an Atlanta resident. Stacey has been the catalyst of many positive changes in Georgia. I am proud to know her and watch her in action.

TWO CHURCHES

I grew up Catholic, but I was feeling an emptiness with religion. I was always spiritual, but was thirsty for inspiration at church. We went to the beautiful Christ the King Cathedral in Buckhead and sent our daughter, Lily, there for elementary school and would try to attend Mass on Sundays (sometimes, but not always). We met some of our best friends when we moved back to Atlanta from Pasadena in a group called the "Young Marrieds." That said, I have been conflicted with the Catholic Church, especially due to its stand on not allowing women to be priests and because of the scandals with some of the priests. It's a subject I have spent a lot of time thinking and praying about. We've tried other churches, some of them very inspirational, but we never felt at home. That ended the day we attended Mass at Our Lady of Lourdes in Old Fourth Ward.

Considered the Mother Church of African American Roman Catholics in Atlanta, Our Lady of Lourdes welcomes all races, cultures, and faiths to our dynamic Mass. Our Lady of Lourdes affectionately calls their worship style the "Lourdes Experience" because at all Masses, even the Saturday vigil, you'll find an upbeat service featuring a variety of music (gospel, spirituals, contemporary Christian, and classics) accompanied by a world class choir led by the Director of Music and Liturgy. Any new people attending Mass are welcomed with a fresh baked loaf of bread.

GUIDE FOR BEING A POSITIVE LIGHT

1. Whose corner can you brighten today?

_____

_____

_____

_____

_____

_____

_____

2. What can you do to make your neighborhood a better place?

_____

_____

_____

_____

_____

_____

_____

JOJO'S GOGO

☐ *Send Our Lady of Lourdes a donation*

LIL' DITTY

Be the spark, when brightening corners of your world,
Your positivity will be observed.
It's always right to be kind and serve,
Shine the light, it's something we deserve.

10 !

Pushing to "Yes And, And"

Am I supposed to say yes?
Am I supposed to say no?

Yes is a powerful word. I love to say "yes." Yes, to an
assignment at work. Yes to a volunteer opportunity. Yes
to a board role on a nonprofit.

Yes, I'll have coffee with you.

Yes, I'll have lunch with you.

Yes, I'll help you find a job.

Yes, I'll write that recommendation letter.

Yes, I'll lead the block party in our neighborhood.

Yes, I'll lead the PR and put my house on the Druid Hills
Tour of Homes.

Yes, we'll go to your party, your party, and your party—all in the same night. It was exhilarating, albeit exhausting. When I went to work at Interface, I traveled almost 80 percent of the time and most of it was globally. There was a natural purge of the boards and volunteer roles because I simply could not do all these things. For three years, I didn't do anything except work and spend time with my immediate family. I will say, that was not good for my soul. It was time for a reset. I had to prioritize what I was passionate about while asking myself what made me excited enough to get me up in the morning. I meditated on it and landed on placing my energy on nonprofits that help children and young professionals who are growing in their careers. I am also very passionate about Atlanta and did agree to serve as the Board Chair for the Atlanta Convention and Visitors Bureau.

Favorite quotes on yes and no:

- "If someone offers you an amazing opportunity but you are not sure you can do it, say yes—then learn how to do it later!" —*Richard Branson*

- "I imagine saying 'yes' is the only living thing."—*e.e. cummings*

- "Say 'yes' and you'll figure it out afterward." —*Tina Fey*

- "What is 'no?' Either you have asked the wrong question or you have asked the wrong person. Find a way to get to the 'yes.'"—*Jeanette Winterson*

- "Take 'no' as an encouragement to redouble his efforts, so it was easier to say 'yes' right away." —*Steig Larsson*

- "Tone is the hardest part of saying no." —*Jonathan Price*

- "You will have to say no to things to say yes to your work. It will be worth it." —*Lin-Manuel Miranda*

ANN CRAMER'S "YES, AND, AND"

I heard this phrase from the great Ann Cramer. Ann is a bright light in Atlanta and a fellow Leadership Atlanta alumna. She now counsels nonprofits with Coxe Curry and Associates after retiring from her role as Director of IBM's Corporate Citizenship and Corporate Affairs for the Americas.

Ann currently serves as chair of Public Broadcasting Atlanta (PBA), the Atlanta Regional Commission (ARC) Educated Subcommittee, the Atlanta Partners for Education (APFE), and as the past chair of the Georgia Partnership for Excellence in Education (GPEE) and the Carter Center Board of Councilors. Ann is currently on the boards of the Community Foundation of Greater Atlanta, the Metro Atlanta Chamber Education Committee, the Governor's Office of Workforce Development, and the Georgia Public Education Foundation. She serves on the Council on Foundations Board, the Woodruff Arts Center Board, the Alliance Theater Company Board, the UGA Board of Visitors, the Hands On Atlanta Advisory Board, the Atlanta Cities of Service Board, Imagine It! The Children's Museum of Atlanta, TechBridge, and CHRIS 180.

I often run into Ann at Leadership Atlanta alumni events and around Atlanta on the Beltline. She always has an ear-to-ear smile and exudes positivity. Her mantra in any situation is "Yes, And."

That said, after I talked to her on a Zoom call, I learned that she uses a "Yes, And, And" philosophy. When Ann started at IBM, she was in charge of their Corporate Citizenship and Corporate Affairs. It was required to call someone back within 24 hours and respond to requests. Through that experience, she developed a graceful way to not say "yes" to every request that came her way, and there were many. Ann said, "Sometimes I had to say 'no,' and I learned in declining the requests how to do so. I would listen and learn, reflect on the situation, and then act."

Here's her approach when she would receive a request from a nonprofit to donate money or volunteer time:

First, she listened and learned about the organization, and she would thank them. Second, she would reflect and ask herself, "How can I help them?" Finally, she would act. Sometimes, it was a "Yes, we can help" and sometimes it was a "no, but here's who I think can help" and then direct the requester to the resource. Those asking for the donation of time or money really appreciated Ann's kindness and generosity. She affirmed and listened and really helped people in need.

I asked Ann how she had said "yes" or "no" today. Ann replied that she uses the same approach for her time, talent, and treasure. She listens, reflects, and gains clarity about whether to accept or decline, and then gives another "yes" on next steps. What a beautiful approach to show others you hear them, you are listening, learning, reflecting, and putting actions in motion.

SHONDA AND PELOTON

Shonda Rhimes' book, *Year of Yes: How to Dance It Out, Stand in the Sun, and Be Your Own Person,* is a must-read. Her TED talk "My year of saying yes to everything" (based on the aforementioned book) inspired me to say "yes" to everything (or most everything) again. Like me, her work gives her the hum. But her family gives her the "real hum." Career awards and compliments are no substitute for family and causes that need love.

The following are some of the key lessons from her TED Talk:

- Say "Yes" to Using Your Voice.
- Say "Yes" to Saying "No".
- Say "Yes" to Real Friendships.
- Say "Yes" to Love.

Peloton has an excellent series called "Year of Yes" and is a collaboration with Rhimes, a fellow Peloton enthusiast. It's an eight-week series of her "Year of Yes" philosophy. She is the genius executive producer and writer behind *Grey's Anatomy, Scandal, How to Get Away with Murder* and *Bridgerton*, among other things.

The "Year of Yes" workouts are four times a week and the instructors are Robin Arzon, Tunde Oyeneyin, Adrean Williams, and Chelsea Jackson Roberts.

Classic Peloton does something for everyone and figures out how to meet its enthusiasts where they are.

Rhimes is continuing to step into her power as an athlete and knows that the act of working out is a practice for building strength, resilience, and confidence. I loved Tunde's class where she stated that sometimes you have to say "hell no" to something so that you can say "hell yes" to something else.

My "hell yes" right now is saying "hell yes" to being there for Lily during her last years in high school, leaving a legacy at my company, serving on the Covenant House Board, and becoming an athlete.

"Put your crown on and remember who you are."
—ROBIN ARZON

IMPROV-ABILITY

In my quest to become a better public speaker, I decided to take an improv class. Improv is the form of theater, most often comedy, in which most of what is performed is unplanned or unscripted. Improv is improvised by the performers based on suggestions from the audience. The dialogue, actions, stories, and characters are created collaboratively by the players as the improvisation unfolds in real time.

There's a great book called *Yes, And* written by Kelly Leonard and Tom Yorton that celebrates the "Yes, And" approach. According to the book, for over 20 years, The Second City Theater has launched the careers of comedians such as Tina Fey and Stephen Colbert. Players master an ability to co-create and build a scene using the "Yes, And" approach.

According the book, these are the seven elements of improv:

▸ Yes, And, by which you give every idea a chance to be acted on

▸ Ensemble, reconciling the needs of individuals with those of a broader team

▸ Co-creation, which highlights the importance of dialogue in creating new products, processes, and relationships

▸ Authenticity, or being unafraid to speak truth to power, challenge convention, or break the rules

▸ Failure, which teaches us that not only is it okay to fail, but we should always include it as part of the process

▸ Follow the Follower, which gives any member of the group the chance to assume the leadership role

▸ Listening, in which you learn to stay in the moment, and understanding the difference between listening to understand and listening to merely respond

These are tenants that can be used in all areas of life. And it's such a blast to practice. Since "yes" is one of my favorite words, I am learning not to say "yes, but" anymore and instead say "Yes, And." It gives others a license to build upon your good idea. It promotes creativity, gives respect to others, and helps drive inspiration and innovation.

GUIDE TO THE "YES, AND" APPROACH

1. Name the areas in your life that you'd like to say "no" to

_____

_____

_____

_____

_____

_____

2. Name the areas you'd like to say "hell yeah" to

_____

_____

_____

_____

_____

_____

3. Fill in the blank: "Yes, And" _____

JOJO'S GOGO

- [ ] *Think deeply before I say "yes" (An invitation does not always need a "Yes" and "No" is a complete sentence)*
- [ ] *Get my coaching certificate*

LIL' DITTY

Learning to change to include "Yes, And."
Thinking through the ask beforehand.
Want to do a good job so things don't get out of hand.
Balance "Yes, and" so that it flows with other demands.

Playlists

*Music is the soundtrack
of your life.*

In my high school yearbook, I stated that my ambition was that I wanted to be a music producer. My teenage years were spent listening to albums, 8-Tracks, and cassettes. That never happened, but I am usually the one who acts as the producer, or the lead of our big corporate meetings where we bring field managers, sales leaders or franchisees together.

I get psyched planning the presentations and figuring out the "walk on" music for the speakers. I am that person in the DJ booth running between the dancers to give the DJ the playlist. I am the first to arrive and the last to leave at a dance party.

When I was in high school, I left the job at McDonald's to become a server at Lil' Rays, a restaurant that served freshly prepared po'boys, oysters on the half-shell, peel-and-eat shrimp and cold bottleneck beer. I always had a pocket full of cash, because the clientele was always happy when they were at Lil' Rays. That cash money afforded me the opportunity to see countless live concerts at the Mississippi Coast Coliseum in Biloxi and the Civic Center in Mobile. I'd venture to guess I saw Van Halen at least 10 times. Same with Jimmy Buffet.

Other notable live concerts I got to attend were the Rolling Stones, the Doobie Brothers, the B-52s, Steely Dan, Tina Turner, Frank Sinatra, Lionel Richie, U2, KISS, The Judds, and Madonna. At the Delta Blues and Heritage Festival, I got to see "Big Daddy" Robinson, James "Son" Thomas, Aaron Neville, Don McLean, Sting, The Police, and Prince.

I finally watched the film, *Muscle Shoals*. It's both a documentary and a tribute to the outlier Alabama city that is home to the FAME Recording Studio where numerous famous bands and musicians recorded their hit songs. Some of these artists include The Rolling Stones, Aretha Franklin, Percy Sledge, and Lynyrd Skynyrd. All I can say is watch it!

I wrote and shared a post on LinkedIn about *Muscle Shoals*, and received so many positive likes and comments. A few recommendations from the LinkedIn posse for other music documentaries are: *Song Exploder*, *Echo in the Canyon*, *Jimmy Carter: Rock & Roll President*, *Standing in the Shadows of Motown* and *The Wrecking Crew*. I can't wait to watch these!

DJ JOJO

One of these days, I'd love to have the DJ equipment so I can set up dance parties at home. In the meantime, (this is just for fun because music is joy) I'll share my playlists for various moods or situations:

DANCE PARTY	MAKING A CHANGE	WORKOUT
I Wanna Dance with Somebody—Whitney Houston	Changes in Latitude-Jimmy Buffet	Pain & Joy—Rob Base and DJ E-Z Rock
Billie Jean-Michael Jackson	Revolution-The Beatles	Jolene-Dolly Parton
Crazy in Love-Beyoncé	I Will Always Love You-Dolly Parton	Bang on the Drum All Day-Todd Rundgren
September-Earth, Wind and Fire	Lovely Day-Bill Withers	I Will Survive-Gloria Gaynor
I'm Coming Out-Diana Ross	Georgia On My Mind-Ray Charles	Jump-Van Halen
Let's Dance-David Bowie	Your Song-Elton John	Start Me Up-The Rolling Stones
I'm So Excited-The Pointer Sisters	Overjoyed-Stevie Wonder	Brian Wilson-Barenaked Ladies
Super Freak-Rick James	You Can't Always Get What You Want-The Rolling Stones	Love Train-The O'Jays
I Feel for You-Chaka Khan	Mrs. Potter's Lullaby Counting Crows	Party Train-The Gap Band
It's Tricky-Run-DMC	If I Ain't You-Alicia Keys	Ain't No Mountain High Enough-Diana Ross
Love Shack-B-52s	See the World-Gomez	Castle on the Hill-Ed Sheeran
Last Dance-Donna Summer	My Love-Paul McCartney	The End-The Beatles

In Jackson, many black musicians stayed at the Summers Hotel and in 1966, the hotel proprietor opened a club in the basement and called it the Subway Lounge. It was a classic juke joint, smoky and filled with people from all walks of life. The Knee Deep Band was the original house band and its vocalist, Walter Lee "Big Daddy" Hood was billed as "500 Pounds of Blues."

Quotes from my heroes on music:

▸ "If you have to ask what jazz is, you'll never know." — *Louis Armstrong*

▸ "As long as we live, there is never enough singing." — *Martin Luther*

▸ "Everybody's life is a soap opera. Everybody's life is a country western song, depends on who's writing it."— *Dolly Parton*

▸ "The blues echoes right through into soul, R&B and hip hop. It's part of the make-up of modern music. You can't turn your back on the blues." —*Ronnie Wood*

GUIDE TO PLAYLISTS

1. What is on your favorite playlist?

_____

_____

_____

_____

_____

_____

_____

_____

_____

_____

_____

2. Download it, sing out loud, and dance like nobody's watching. When you are feeling blue, music and a dance party cure all.

JOJO'S GOGO

- [ ] *Learn how to be a DJ*
- [ ] *Download every number one song of the week for every year of my life*

LIL' DITTY

Music has always been my companion,
Never missing a live concert was my pastime,
Music fills my soul and helps through the climb,
Enjoy writing poems and songs that rhyme!

12 !

Pathfinder—Good Goes Around

Wanderlust.

I am a Delta Million Miler. I learned, by traveling to China many times, as well as Thailand, Mexico, Italy, France, Germany, Spain, Mexico, and Peru, to appreciate the cultural differences. My favorite thing to do is walk around a city early in the morning and appreciate its beauty and uniqueness, sit in a piazza or square, enjoy a cup of coffee, and meet the locals.

Jeff Hilimire shared his favorite quote, and I agree with its message.

"Everyone wants to live on top of the mountain, but all the happiness and growth occurs while you're climbing it.

—ANDY ROONEY

Rooney offers great perspective on appreciating life's journey. Here are some of my other favorite quotes on the importance of new experiences, especially as they relate to travel:

- "Once a year, go someplace you've never been before."—*Dalai Lama*

- "It's better to travel well than arrive."—*Buddha*

- "Traveling—it leaves you speechless, then turns you into a storyteller." —*Ibn Battuta*

- "Paris is always a good idea."—*Audrey Hepburn's character in* Sabrina

BEIJING

When I went to Beijing as a grad student, I took in the city with my classmates. We rode in a rickshaw, went to the Beijing Zoo (where I got my wallet stolen), and walked around Tiananmen Square. My classmates, Joanne, Karen, and my friend, Louise, who tagged along, were tired the last day. Determined to walk the Great Wall of China, I went alone, and I am so glad I did.

Behind me, walking up the wall was a very dapper couple in their late 50s. I marveled over their snappy outfits and determination. When I finally reached my destination, I wanted a photo to remember it by. With my small Canon digital camera, I asked the couple if they would mind taking my photo. The woman remarked, "Why, it would be a pleasure." Aha! I recognized that accent and asked where she was from.

She replied, "We are Dr. and Mrs. Dewey Lane and we are from Pascagoula, Mississippi."

I couldn't believe it! "Well, I am Jo Ann Streiff Herold, and I am from Ocean Springs, Mississippi."

You see, Ocean Springs is only 25 minutes from Pascagoula on the Mississippi coast. We furthered our conversation where I continued, "My college roommate, Mimi Robinson, is from Pascagoula, do you know her?"

Mrs. Lane said, "Why, yes, Harold and Dr. Lane were medical partners." We had a good talk after that and I was excited to meet someone in a faraway place who was from so close to home.

But the story continues—the following weekend, in Pascagoula, Dr. and Mrs. Dewey Lane saw my best friend's parents, Sue and Moreno Jones, from Ocean Springs, at a party and replayed our chance meeting on the Great Wall. The Jones told the Lanes about our many travels together and how I was like a daughter to them when their daughter Susan and I were growing up. I was Susan's maid of honor in her wedding. Dr. Dewey Lane then called my mom to tell her that he just had to let her know about all of the mutual connections around the globe.

On that same trip, Louise and I went to the Beijing Zoo. Louise is obsessed with pandas and I agreed to go with her. China does not have the same queuing system as we do in the US. In the middle of the mob getting into the zoo, I felt someone reach into my bag. Once we were out of the crowd, I immediately checked my bag and my wallet had been stolen, including my driver's license, credit cards, cash, and my library card. Fortunately, I had left my passport in the safe at the hotel. I was forced to borrow money from my friends for incidentals on our next few days in China until I could get to a cash machine at home and pay them back.

What I hadn't realized is that the outlets do not use the same voltage in China as in the U.S. I plugged in my curling iron and burned off a chunk of my hair. There is nothing like the smell of burning hair in a small hotel room. The trip to China had its highs and lows—mostly highs—and I wouldn't trade it for any experience in the world.

The next time I was in China, I was met by Sunny Wang, a colleague from Interface. Sunny was my personal tour guide, proudly showing me Shanghai, Wuhan, and lots of cities in between. She told me about the cultural revolution from 1966 to 1976, we shared whole crabs, and Sunny howled with laughter as I was eating them. We visited the Shanghai Interface office and visited customers all over China.

Sunny and I became fast friends. She's even been to Atlanta and looked into sending her daughter, Emily, to a private high school here, as we agreed to be Emily's host family. She and I text and catch up as often as possible, looking forward to our next reunion.

THE AMAZON

A few years after we got married, Mark and I embarked on an adventure to go down the Amazon River. We went with our friends, Monica, Gil, Laura, Rob, Al and Darcy. The trip was billed as a cruise, but it was really a big fishing boat that took us down the enormous river.

The good news is that the fishing boat had a bar! We drank dollar Cristal beers until they ran out and got more. On the boat, we met Francisco Grippa, a jolly Peruvian who loved fine wine and to paint beautiful scenes from the Amazon on bark. We went to his gallery in Pevas, Peru, a small town on the Amazon River where he still lives and paints today. Mark and I purchased a beautiful painting with the cacophony of colors of the Amazon River. I still smile when I see that painting in my living room.

The Amazon trip was mind-blowing for me. We learned about the destruction of the rainforests, the ecology, and would listen to the sounds of the wildlife and insects singing at night. We visited a zoo on the Amazon, held an anaconda snake, swam in the Amazon River, ate the local food given to us on the boat, visited a shaman, and went to a tribe. We were humbled when we visited a leper colony.

I was struck by the poverty of the people when we would stop in the villages on our cruise down the Amazon. I was also equally struck by how happy everyone seemed—especially the children. Seems like money doesn't buy happiness. I wouldn't trade these memories for anything in the world.

TRAVEL TIPS

Traveling has enabled me to get out of my bubble, to see new perspectives, to eat great food, get to know some pretty amazing people, and to see some beautiful sites. Here are a few tips I have for traveling, especially internationally:

Go local:

▸ Go to the local cafés, farmers markets, and restaurants.

▸ Eat the local yogurt and honey. It will help your digestion and immunity.

▸ Laugh a lot, take lots of photos, and talk to people.

▸ Read the news about what is going on in the country before you travel.

▸ See the sites, but visit only one church and one museum per day.

- Walk, instead of taking the train, in the airport. Helps you get more steps and you can usually see airport art.

- Take the stairs to the tops of the churches. The views are better.

- Bring your journal and document the trip. Post photos—you'll enjoy them later.

- Send postcards. Buy postcards and place them in your memory book.

- Go to the local pub at night—make friends at the bar!

- Take the tours. They typically give a good overview of the city and provide a quick history lesson.

- Stay in nice hotels. Get to know your hotel team and ask for their recommendations on places to see and go.

- Know that the toilets, the outlets, and how to turn on the lights in your hotel room are all unique to the country.

- Bring the local adapter for your laptop, phone, etc.

- Get local currency so you have cash on hand. Use your American Express for all other expenses.

- Buy local art—you will also have a memento from your trip and it helps to tell a story.

- See the sites at night. I'll always remember seeing the Eiffel Tower at twilight.

Stay Healthy:

- Bring and take multivitamins, lysine, and vitamin C packages.

- Drink a lot of water on the plane.

- Get lots of sleep, then get on local time.

- Bring some Kind or RX bars in your bag for nourishment.

- Bring comfortable walking shoes. Bring fun shoes for the evening.

- Plan ahead and enjoy!

- Read and plan, get attraction or concert tickets in advance, but leave free time to wander.

- Recognize that while the settings are different, humans are the same around the globe. Most people are in love with love, value family, and their loved ones.

- Travel big and bring the clothes and shoes you love. Check your bag so that you don't have luggage in the airport, while keeping anything valuable (jewelry) and important (medication and passport) on your person.

- Make a copy of your driver's license and passport and leave a copy at home in case you lose it when traveling.

- Appreciate and celebrate the differences in climate, dialect, and food. Don't judge because it's different, instead appreciate the differences and embrace them.

GUIDE FOR
SEEING THE WORLD !

1. What are the top three places on your bucket list?

_____

_____

_____

2. Start planning!

_____

_____

_____

_____

_____

_____

_____

_____

_____

_____

_____

JOJO'S GO-GO

- ☐ *Visit the national parks in the U.S.*
- ☐ *Visit Greece, Africa, Europe*
- ☐ *Go on trips for destination weddings, birthdays, anniversaries with friends when invited*

LIL' DITTY

Oh, the places in the world we'll go,
The pandemic has made travels slow.
Keep memories of adventures in my mind,
Pining to take a break from the grind,
Looking forward to Europe and having a great time.

13

Purpose to Serve Others

Do great things on purpose.

I am in the hospitality industry where our main goal is to serve others. It fits me and my philosophies. There's been a lot written on servant leadership and I want to give my perspective on it.

For servant leaders, it's more of a calling than a job. Servant leaders consider leadership positions as a privilege and strive for the "we" over the "me." Dan McAleenan, the Chief Operating Officer at HoneyBaked, is someone who practices and studies servant leadership.

TRADITIONAL LEADER	SERVANT LEADER
Leadership is a rank to obtain	Leadership is an opportunity to serve others
Leverages power and control to drive results	Leverages power and control to drive engagement
Measures results though output	Measures success through growth and development
Speaks	Listens

Servant leaders believe their job is to serve the teams and do so by:

▸ Clarifying the purpose or the "why" behind the "what."

▸ Doing the right thing.

▸ Providing good direction by listening, then leading.

▸ Working together as a team to help problem solve.

▸ Honoring their commitments, showing up on time, and providing their deliverables on time.

▸ Listening empathetically to those they lead, respecting that there will be different perspectives.

▸ Going beyond what is asked of them, providing motivation and extra touches.

Favorite Quotes on Purpose:

▸ "We make a living by what we get. We make a life by what we give." —*Winston Churchill*

▸ "As we look ahead into the next century, leaders will be those who empower others."—*Bill Gates*

▸ "Organizations exist to serve. Period. Leaders live to serve. Period."—*Tom Peters*

▸ "True leadership must be for the benefit of the followers, not the enrichment of the leaders."—*John C. Maxwell*

MEET RODNEY BULLARD

Rodney was my introduction partner for Leadership Atlanta. What that means is that before the year starts, the two introduction partners need to meet and coordinate on a three-minute skit to introduce the other person.

At the time, Rodney was serving as an assistant United States attorney prosecuting complex criminal cases. For his service, the United States Attorney General presented him with the Department of Justice Director's Award.

And, I was at Arby's. What the Leadership Atlanta organizers did not know was that Rodney was about to go work at Chick-fil-A to lead their community engagement, philanthropic, and sustainability strategy and become the Executive Director of the Chick-fil-A Foundation. We had a hilarious skit about the cows and curly fries and became fast friends.

Rodney also previously served at the Pentagon as a Congressional legislative liaison in the Office of the Secretary of the Air Force. He is an alumnus of the Air Force Academy, Duke Law School, the University of Georgia's Terry College of Business and Harvard Business School's Advanced Management Program.

Rodney epitomizes servant leadership. In his book *Heroes Wanted*, Rodney provides an in-depth perspective on leadership, service and personal development. He tells heartfelt stories on how to make an impact in the community and beyond. The best advice Rodney has ever gotten is, "you are more than enough."

Rodney's favorite quote is a Bible verse from Proverbs 31:8-9, "Speak up for those who can't speak for themselves and see that they get justice." I adore Rodney and am grateful for the example he sets.

PAY IT FORWARD

The pay-it-forward concept is not new. According to Wikipedia, the concept dates back to 317 BC where it was a key plot point in a play in ancient Athens. It became hugely popular in the 2000 movie of the same name and has become a philosophy principle.

At its heart, to "pay it forward" is when someone does something for you, instead of paying that person back directly, you pass it on to another person.

The reason I like to use this principle is that kindness can build a community and one good deed deserves another.

WAYS TO PAY IT FORWARD

Practice Kindness:

▸ Compliment the first three people you talk to today.

▸ Send a positive text to five different people right now.

▸ Handwrite inspirational notes and distribute them to your neighbors.

▶ Email or write to someone who has made a difference in your life, perhaps a teacher. Post it on Facebook. It will make their day and will make yours.

▶ Put your phone away in the company of others. Practice mindfulness.

▶ Try to make sure everyone in the conversation is heard.

▶ Write a gratitude and kindness list each day in your journal.

Give:

▶ Donate old blankets to a homeless shelter.

▶ Surprise a neighbor with brownies.

▶ When a waiter does a good job, overtip and tell the manager.

▶ Leave goodies out front for the UPS and mail couriers.

▶ Smile and say hello to everyone you see today.

▶ Donate when someone has a fundraiser for a cause. Your support means the world to them and it's a win-win.

My favorite "pay it forward" quotes:

▶ "The point is not to pay back kindness, but to pass it on." —*Julia Alvarez*

▶ "Carry out a random act of kindness with no expectation of reward, safe in the knowledge that one day, someone might do the same for you." —*Princess Diana*

I admire servant leaders and strive to be one daily. I am also striving to pay it forward. It's about setting direction and helping others succeed. It's so rewarding to see a direct report receive a promotion, or help a former colleague get a big new job or serve in the community—and what is better than that?

GUIDE TO SERVANT LEADERSHIP

1. Who can I help today?

_____

_____

_____

_____

2. How can I serve them?

_____

_____

_____

_____

3. How can I pay it forward today?

_____

_____

_____

_____

JOJO'S GOGO

- [ ] *Donate to the homeless in a way that is meaningful by giving food boxes with $5 included*
- [ ] *Visit and bring food to elderly neighbor*

LIL' DITTY

Compassion is always welcome,
Serving others is a piece of heaven.
Be the one professing this progression,
Kindness and giving are such a blessing.

14

Practice Joy, Feel Happiness

You are the CEO of joy and happiness for you.

Happiness depends on ourselves. I heard a motivational speaker say, "If you want to be happy, then be happy." Joy is a practice, while happiness is a feeling, meaning it is something you need to work towards every day. The only person who can make you happy is you.

I used to believe that happiness was a destination; something to be obtained once I got married, or received that great promotion, or got a new house. I used to think if we lived in Atlanta or Pasadena that would make me happier. If only we had more money, a boat, could go on that vacation, or whatever.

WHAT'S THE DIFFERENCE BETWEEN JOY AND HAPPINESS?

According to Brainly, "Joy is more consistent and is cultivated internally. It comes when you make peace with who you are, why you are here, and how you are, whereas happiness tends to be externally triggered and based on people, places, things, thoughts, and events."

Happiness is external, whereas joy is internal. They are similar, but two very different emotions.

Ally Love, one of my favorite Peloton instructors, has an amazing "Sundays with Love" class all around the virtues of joy.

JOY	HAPPINESS
Internal	External
In spite of...	As a result of...
Unconditional	Conditional
Independent	Dependent

20 TIPS FOR A JOYOUSLY HAPPY LIFE

Joy is a feeling of great pleasure and happiness. The best days are the ones filled with laughter. When you do things that are good for the soul, you will feel joy. Things like calling an old friend and playing back funny stories, or watching an old episode of *Friends* with a family member and laughing. Mark Twain said, "To get the full value of joy, you must have someone to divide it with."

Dopamine plays a role in how we feel pleasure. Dopamine is a happy, feel-good hormone, and an important part of your brain's reward system. It's a big part of our unique human ability to think and plan. It helps us strive, focus, and find things interesting.

I've done a lot of studying on this subject as happiness is the goal that everyone strives for, right? Through this journey, I have learned that these are the 20 keys to happiness:

1. Connections and relationships are key. As humans, we are hardwired to be with others. And this is not about finding your "soulmate" or romantic relationships; being happy through our posse and friends who are positive and support you can bring happiness and joy in life.

2. Being kind brings personal joy and happiness. Doing something nice for someone else gives our brain a boost and generates a sense of well-being and satisfaction. When I see a homeless person on the street when I am driving, I give them $20. I overtip the valet and watch his or her expression.

3. Whether it's counting your blessings or expressing gratitude, acknowledging the good things in life contributes to your well-being. Material things are only important if they have meaning, such as the book that my dad gave me, a painting from my grandmother, or the art from a trip that we took.

4. Meaning, purpose, and believing that there is something beyond me and larger than my existence helps ground me. I've been walking a lot more lately and paying more attention to the nature surrounding me. And I've started finding feathers on my walkabouts. It's simply amazing when I see them, a burst of joy that explodes in my brain. I will carefully pick up and put the feather in my pocket. Each of these beautiful feathers are then placed in my Michael Hyatt *Full Focus Planner* (I promise, I don't work for them—just love the tool). I read that when you find a feather, it's God's way of showing you that he hears your prayers and dreams, and they will be answered. A beautiful and spiritual symbol on a mindful walk.

5. Making healthy choices is certainly a tenet of happiness. Simple things like eating well, getting enough sleep, and exercise are the key. As I am writing this, we are in the middle of the pandemic. During this time of social distancing, I have rediscovered the joys of cooking. I've been plowing into old cookbooks and have been learning more about the *Blue Zones* way of life. Much has been written about this way of life and I recommend the TED talk on it, *The Blue Zones Kitchen* cookbook, and the Netflix series *Down to Earth with Zac Efron*, a great show on travel, culture, and healthier eating featuring wellness expert, Darin Olien. When I am feeling tired, I'll pop a piece of dark chocolate, as it's a delicious treat and has all kinds of health benefits.

6. Where possible, cut the stressors out of your life. These are things like working outside of work hours, staying out of traffic during rush hour, or not overcommitting on your calendar. When I get angry about something, I try to do something about it. When I get angry with someone, I think deeply about the root of my anger and whether I should thoughtfully say something to them or let it go. Regardless, I will sleep on it before saying something, because I know words matter. And most people don't make me angry, but if they do, it's because I care about them. And because I care about them, I want to choose what I say carefully.

7. There's nothing wrong with a good happy hour (drinking in moderation) now and then. Chardonnay is my happy hour beverage of choice and it's a fun way to unwind, kick my feet up, and laugh with Mark or a friend. Play fun music and have a dance party.

8. Keep learning, keep growing. Right now, I am interested in living a healthy lifestyle and am devouring content in that arena. I'm also interested in coaching and mentoring, and am studying about how to continue to master this subject.

9. Mentioning the benefits of exercise, stretching and doing some quick arm exercises with weights will help to get the blood flowing. I love my Apple Watch. The alerts let me know when to stand up, breathe, and track exercise. Before I had the watch, I was slouched at my desk banging away

on PowerPoint presentations and documents. Because of the tracking, I stand more at my kitchen counter while creating documents for work.

10. Surround yourself with people you love and who love you back. Spend time and hang out with family and friends through food, exercise, binge-watching a TV show, or sports. Life is so much richer when it's shared with others.

11. Find a nonprofit or cause that feeds your soul and give your time and, if you have it, your treasure. Whenever I am feeling down, volunteerism is a salvation that reminds me about the blessings I have.

12. Intently listen to what the other person has to say. Make no judgments and acknowledge how they are feeling. Only offer advice if they ask for it. I am working hard to do this with my daughter. As I am sure she'd attest, I am a work in progress on this one.

13. Seek beauty from the everyday. Look for the beautiful tree, the garden, absorb the weather when it's beautiful, and look at the raindrops when it pours. Go to the beach or the water, and marvel in our sweet earth and God's beauty.

14. As my sister Blake says, "If you don't like the view, find a new chair." With that, it could be looking for an inspiring career, a new sport, getting in shape, or whatever it takes to get the front row seat and a glorious view.

15. Love today and love every day. Love being alive and live it as if it were your last day. Have you ever wondered if it's better to love or to be loved? I love loving—it's active, present and beautiful. That said, the best is when you love and the other person loves you back. Say, "I love you" freely and often, and let those you love know how much you love them. Give big hugs—even if they are virtual.

16. Make your bed every day. If you make your bed, you've accomplished the first task of the day and it shows that even little things matter. During the day, when you walk into your bedroom, it will look neater and tidier. And, you get to crawl in at night to a freshly made bed after a hard day. Keep your space filled with cut flowers and green plants. It will make your home beautiful, smell nice, and may improve the air quality in your home.

17. Fill your brain with positivity. I used to watch a lot of scary true crime shows and I do love them. That said, I was having trouble sleeping and it was making me anxious. I did a detox from those scary shows and started watching movies and programs that were more positive or funny. Movies like *Night School, The Hangover, Bridesmaids* and *The Blind Side,* and series like *The Queen's Gambit* and *The Crown.*

18. Get a massage as often as you can afford and time allows. Massages have so many benefits, including helping to destress, relaxation, improved skin tone, and they just help feed the soul.

19. Certain foods bring joy. If I am ever feeling blue, I'll stop by my local Kale Me Crazy and get an acai bowl with blueberries, strawberries, or honey. I also know it's going to be a good day when I can stop by Starbucks and grab a low-fat latte.

20. When times get really tough, take time off. Sometimes it's good to walk away from a situation and take a break. Do things to rejuvenate the soul, such as walking, vacationing, going out for a nice dinner, or getting a facial. I've found that when I do that, I am better able to embrace the tough situation and help myself and others.

Oprah Winfrey writes, "Joy is one part inner peace, one part giddy delight, and 100 percent attainable." The commonality in the human experience is the same. We have the same sorrows, the same triumphs. Joy is joy is joy.

Ally Love, Peloton instructor extraordinaire says, "You can be in a mess, but you can't stay in the mess." Feel pain, but don't suffer.

MY FAVORITE JOY QUOTES

▸ "Find joy in everything you choose to do. Every job, relationship, home…it's your responsibility to love it, or change it." –*Chuck Palahniuk*

▸ "Let your joy be in your journey, not in some distant goal." –*Tim Cook*

▸ "Sometimes your joy is the source of your smile, but sometimes your smile can be the source of your joy." – *Thich Nhat Hanh*

MY FAVORITE HAPPINESS QUOTES

▶ "There is only one happiness in life. To love and be loved."
  –George Sand

▶ "Happiness lies in the joy of achievement and the thrill
  of creative effort." *–Franklin D. Roosevelt*

▶ "Spread love everywhere you go. Let no one ever come to
  you without leaving happier." *–Mother Teresa*

▶ "Happiness is when what you think, what you say, and
  what you do are in harmony." *–Mahatma Gandhi*

▶ "Only I can change my life. No one can do it for me." *–
  Carol Burnett*

▶ "Happiness is the new rich. Inner peace is the new success.
  Health is the new wealth. Kindness is the new cool." *–
  Syed Balkhi*

GUIDE TO JOY AND HAPPINESS

1. Describe a time when you've been happy. What was the setting? Who was there? How did you feel?

   _____

   _____

   _____

   _____

   _____

   _____

2. Are you happy? If not, what is holding you back?

   _____

   _____

   _____

   _____

   _____

   _____

JOJO'S GOGO

☐ *Write New Year's cards to others*
☐ *Exercise four days a week*

LIL' DITTY

Walking on sunshine and today will be just fine,
Sending joy all the time.
Noting beauty while I make the climb,
Celebrating with music and fine wine.

15

Pastimes and Legacy

Looking at the past in order to look ahead.

s I look ahead, I also look back and smile on the younger me. My years in Ocean Springs were filled with learning values, building lifelong friendships, identifying my talents and strengths, and learning who I am and who I am not. I went back to my younger self so that I could look forward.

MY 20s

My 20s were filled with a desire for accomplishment at work, dating and then getting married to Mark. It was a time of growth for me. I was not at peace during my 20s. I think the safe space of Ocean Springs and Mississippi State didn't quite prepare me for adulthood. I started at the bottom in a low-level position and wasn't making much money. My perfectionism was not always my best friend during this time. The good news is I didn't give up, I kept doing good work, building relationships, using my Covey planner, and setting goals. I did take risks by taking on new jobs and charting a path for myself. I remember being very melancholy about turning 30 as I hadn't achieved the goals I had charted out—like writing a book or getting an MBA.

MY 30s

The Covey planner motivated me to drive over to Mercer University to inquire about getting an MBA. Serendipitously, I was able to get in to see the Director of the MBA program and I signed up on the spot. The MBA came at the perfect time. I had the work experience now and the theory behind the education made perfect sense. It ultimately became a game changer for me and enabled me to teach.

Mark and I also moved to Pasadena for his job at Avery Dennison. This was such a fun time in our marriage. I consulted with The Honey Baked Ham Company and other startups in Los Angeles. Mark had a 10-minute commute to his office near the Rose Bowl. The weather was always perfect and we made some of our best friends who are still our best friends. We ultimately moved back home to Atlanta and I am so incredibly grateful for that time on the West Coast.

HoneyBaked recruited me back to the brand and my career kept growing with them. Time went so swiftly, and Mark and I wanted to have a family. When I learned I couldn't get pregnant, we immediately started the adoption process. From start to finish the adoption process was nine months. Lily was probably being conceived as we started the paperwork. There are so many ways that God winked while we were adopting Lily. To tell you a bit about Lily, she is a happy, outgoing, bubbly, and wise soul. I love her with my heart and soul, and am so proud to call her my daughter.

We got involved with our Atlanta neighbors on Oakdale Road and our Christ the King Marrieds Group became our family. I got super involved in the Atlanta community, especially with the American Marketing Association.

MY 40s

I left HoneyBaked and started my own consultancy. That was hard! I learned that I really missed being with a team and I love working for iconic brands. Lucky for me, I ran into Hala Moddelmog when she returned to Atlanta after her stint as CEO of Susan G. Komen for the Cure. Hala had just accepted the role as President of Arby's Restaurant Group and she had a role open. I interviewed and got the job! I loved working for Arby's, loved the energy, and being a part of the turnaround team. I worked with some of the brightest and best in the industry, and was given some very plum assignments.

Hala sponsored me for Leadership Atlanta and, after my third attempt to get in, I was finally accepted. At the same time, I was also serving as the President of the Atlanta chapter of the American Marketing Association. Needless to say, with a demanding full-time job, volunteer work, along with being a mom and having a family, I was very, very busy.

During this time, I got a call from Lisa Lilienthal, who is a longtime consultant for Interface. Their CEO, Dan Hendrix, wanted to learn more about how marketing works in a consumer-driven brand. Interface was very sales driven, but had not had a strong marketing presence. Dan, Lisa and I met, and Dan and I had a great connection. I told him I'd take a stab at the job description. I ended up putting my name in the hat for the role. After about eight interviews and a three-hour conversation with an industrial psychologist, I got the job. My first week in the role was speaking to the team in Europe about why I wanted to work at Interface.

The role was global and I learned about working across all time zones, traveling about 80 percent of the time. I loved learning the entirely new-to-me business of flooring and getting to meet people from around the globe. I loved that the company had a strong purpose and mission, and a strong brand in their market-place. Because of all the travel, I wasn't as involved in the Atlanta community. During my time there, all I really could handle was work and family. I'll always be appreciative of that experience. That said, at a certain point, it was time for me to walk away and am glad I did it when I did.

At the time, Lily was going to a new school and going into the seventh grade. I wanted to be there, be at home, and reconnect with our neighbors and community.

MY 50s

After a very fun stint as the Interim Chief Marketing Officer at Tropical Smoothie Café with one of my favorite people, Mike Rotondo, as CEO, I returned back to HoneyBaked after eight years. I've gotten much more grounded in who I am—good and bad, perfections and imperfections—and spend a lot of time mapping out the next 50 years. And it's all about purpose, passion, and the posse.

I am finally writing this book, after having it as a goal for over 30 years. Writing this book has stirred up so many memories and so many emotions. I've gone back to old journals, old Covey planners, old photos and tried to dig deep. And who am I writing it for? I am writing it for Lily, for anyone who will read it, but mostly for myself.

I've pulled out books that provided inspiration. Matthew McConaughey's book *Greenlights* is one of the best, freshest, and most authentic books I've read. And, you know how much I love quotes, so I am sharing these favorites from his book:

- ▸ "Be less impressed, more involved."
- ▸ "Alright, alright, alright."
- ▸ "Knowing who we are is hard. Eliminate who we're not first, and we'll find ourselves where we need to be."
- ▸ "Sometimes we don't need advice. Sometimes we just need to hear we are not the only ones."
- ▸ "We don't live longer when we try not to die, we live longer when we're too busy living."

JOJO'S GOGO

- [ ] *Journal your decades*
- [ ] *Read and listen to inspirational books and podcasts*
- [ ] *Write your own ending*

LIL' DITTY

Rocking the decades, learning along way,
Purpose and passion rule the day.
Family, friends and travel are life's bouquet,
A fine cheese tray and Veuve Clicquot!

16 !

Prepping for the Next 50 Years—26 Million Minutes

Time to plan.

I am obsessed with time. It's a precious resource, the great equalizer, and something that everyone has the same amount of in a day. Time is egalitarian. When someone says that they don't have enough time, they are really saying that this is not a priority for them.

WHAT WOULD YOU DO IF YOU WON THE LOTTERY?

My dad's second cousin, David Stacks, won $13 million playing the slots. After he won the money, he and wife Janis changed three things. First, they bought an eight-slot toaster so they could put more bread in to be toasted, got a new fence, and upgraded their car to a Cadillac. Beyond that, nothing changed. They kept their same friends and lived in their same house in a very middle-class neighborhood in Gulfport. They showed up every year for the Christmas Eve family party, laughing, drinking, and joking with their loved ones. They continued to enjoy playing the slots and never changed their friends or their situation.

There was recently a Powerball jackpot and Mark and I bought a ticket. We went back and forth on what we would change if we won and agreed that not a whole lot would change. Mark would probably get a new car (he drives a 10-year-old car), I would get an automatic cappuccino machine, we'd travel more, but that's about it.

I hope to live another 50 years and that is 26,280,000 minutes. Sounds like a lot, but if it goes as quickly as my first 50, it's not too much time. I plan to use it wisely.

Have you heard the song by Tim McGraw, "Live Like You Were Dying"?

The lyrics are powerful words from a powerful performer, with this song and those words running through my brain often. It's amazing when I think about the next chapter in life through these lenses. While I am not going to write a song, I am going to write out what I want to do more of. I am doing this for me and hoping any readers will hold me accountable. Age is the one thing that goes up, but never comes down. I want to get younger, the older I get.

So, here goes and here's how I want to spend my next 26 million minutes:

I am going to **love** more. Starting at home with my precious family whom I love so much. Lily is heading to college soon, and I want these minutes to go slowly. I want to create more family dinners and experiences with my posse. I'm going to live out my purpose to lead with love. What this means is to love my friends in my neighborhood, to lead with love at work—-especially when it comes to honest conversations. I am also going to put my heart and soul into community work at Covenant House to help homeless youth.

Say **"hell no"** more often, so I can say **"hell yes"** more and change my vernacular to "Yes, And." I want to be purposeful and passionate about the things I say "yes" to. When I get the little sick feeling in my pit, that is a "no." When my brain dances with endorphins about an idea, that is a "hell yes."

I want to **see** more. The feather project showed me how much I've been missing on my walks and how much beauty there is in nature. I also want to go see things—concerts, art exhibits, and museums. I want to see my parents, siblings, nieces, nephews, and in-laws more. Time is going too fast and no one is getting any younger. On my bucket list is to see Paul McCartney and Stevie Wonder live.

Speaking of walking, I love to **exercise**. My walks by myself are moments of great reflection and clarity. When I walk with friends, it's such a special way to get to know them better, talk about deep things while seeing the neighborhood and getting exercise. I've recently been walking with Sue Sullivan—she's a gorgeous, soulful lady. She's a historian and real estate agent. On our walks, she tells me about the homes, the history, and the people who live there. I savor my walks with Sue. The Peloton crew has literally changed my life. I look forward to these positive and productive classes with my Peloton family. Also, my workouts with Karyn, Julie, and Reggie are treasured times.

I can't wait to be transported to new destinations and **travel** more. There are so many jaw-dropping places in the United States. I've never seen the Grand Canyon or Alaska. Mark and I will get a small Airstream, take off, and see America. I want to see all the places in the Blue Zones, including Loma Linda in California. The international places of Sardinia, Okinawa, Nicoya, and Ikaria, Machu Picchu, Africa and Tibet are also high on my list.

I want to do a walkabout and see the countryside in England and Ireland. Oh yeah, and I want to go to a live Peloton class in New York. Hell yes.

While I am such a dork at it, I want to play **tennis** more. I've never really played a sport that requires hand-eye coordination, except when I was younger and played catcher for Durbin's softball team in Ocean Springs. I want to be an athlete. It's been such a joy to learn a new skill and I've met so many nice people in my Tennis 101 classes and Saturday clinics. I'll never be a great player, but I do want to become good enough to be on a team, play, get to know other people, and just have fun.

The **five-minute favors** have become a part of my daily life. Adam Grant's *Give and Take* is a must-read. I love helping others become successful and five-minute favors are food for the brain and the soul. Today, I am helping an entrepreneur with a smart product launch link up with a young social media pro to help get the product off the ground. I want to surprise and delight people through random acts of kindness—it could be a handwritten letter, a donation in their name, or an unsolicited introduction.

I want to talk less and actively **listen more**. Instead of jumping in and giving my point of view or opinion, I am going to try to listen deeply. I want to listen to understand, not to respond. I will put my phone down and be present for conversations. I want to train my brain to actively listen to the other person, not wander off in other places in my head. I am going to let them finish their thoughts and ask questions, so that I can genuinely understand.

I am saying "hell yes" and going to class reunions, girls trips, weddings and showers and other **life events**. I've been able to reconnect with my Delta Gamma sisters at a reunion that DG hosted to celebrate their 50 years at Mississippi State. There were 750 alumni and college students rocking the room. It makes me tear up just writing this. It was an amazing gift—one that you only dream of having. Now, if there's a way for me to reconnect with old friends who share so many memories, I am in.

Good friends are a source of love and support. Friends are good for the soul and they are the gift that keeps giving. In the cookie of life, best friends are the chocolate chips. And life is meant to be devoured with best friends and fun adventures. We love to entertain and the sweetest times in our lives are preparing delicious foods, decanting the wine, turning on the playlist, lighting the candles, and letting the laughter happen. I want to have good friends, and most importantly, **be a good friend.**

"A sweet friend refreshes the soul."

—PROVERBS 27:9

I want to **make an impact**, and not be just good at my job, but great at my job. I want any business I work with to be better off because I was there and left a lasting legacy. I want to be a great servant leader for my team and the many customers I serve. I want the business I work with to go beyond profits and serve the communities where we live. Whether it's through support of food banks, or having a big heart when a fellow employee is down and out, those are the businesses that I want to be with. I am very grateful to say that I work for a business who shares my purpose in this area and am very thankful.

Living cleaner is high on the list. During the pandemic, I rediscovered the joy of cooking healthier. I loved cooking on Sundays and packing super healthy meals for the week that can be popped into the microwave and easily enjoyed later. Dan Buettner's *The Blue Zones Kitchen* is my cooking bible. I am cutting back on the caffeine, replacing it with more water and healthy teas. Moreover, I am learning more about sleeping better. The Peloton has a series on sleeping and I have used these before sleep. Most important, doing my part to recycle, using less plastic, and conserving our beautiful planet.

Learning is key and consuming audiobooks, actual books, TED talks, and podcasts are part of my ritual. The content available is vast and inspiring. At the moment, I am obsessed with music documentaries, diving in on rainy days to watch and be amazed.

Standing up, standing out, putting on my big girl pants, and being a **HoneyDragon** are at the top of the list. Being brave and bold, coupled with transparency, authenticity, and actively participating in issues that I believe in, will be in my 26 million minutes. All the while, I want to continue the happiness, joy, gratitude and positivity practice and continue to journal about these topics. Finally, I want to show up and be out in the world, leave a good impression and a positive lasting legacy.

So, that's it. I am going to keep myself honest, and I hope you'll also keep me honest. I have loved writing this book. And as Kat Cole said, "I trust the next chapter of this book, because I know the author."

JOJO'S GOGO

- [ ] *Write your next chapter. Begin with the end in mind. How do you want to lead your next chapter?*
- [ ] *Post your bucket list. Enlist others to add theirs!*

LIL' DITTY

26 million minutes is not a lot.
Time is something I really don't want it to end.
Loving, traveling, exercising and being a great friend,
Making an impact is the currency I'll spend.
Speaking out while living cleaner is my intent,
Getting younger as I age will be a godsend.

The (W)rap Up !

It's been a privilege to write this. Consider this the wrap up—or my rap on life.

THE LIL' DITTY (W)RAP UP

Do what you love and love what you do.
This is so important as you choose,
When you do that, you will never lose.
You'll never be working, which is the best.
Follow your passions, I can attest.
Do things on purpose, cast your vision,
Follow your dreams, that is your mission.
Strong spirit and a humble heart is so lit,
You'll be too legit to quit.
Should I stay, should I go? Only I know.
Should I move up, move over, or move out?
Look for signals, they are always about.

It's about doing nothing, or a change.
Advice from a friend or prayer help rearrange,
To provide clarity, when it's time to make a change.
The people around me make it more fun,
I'll never regret spending time when I am done.
No one wishes they spent more time working,
When you can be with your cherished ones.
Life is better with the people you love in the sun.
Be the one who chose to go for it,
Have determination, grace and grit.
Do what you love and go for it,
With a good plan and strength not to quit.
Be who you are, and you will go far,
Be kind, authentic, always raising the bar.
Be authentic, be your own North Star.
Have a HoneyDragon spirit and be who you are.
It's OK to fake it till you make it,
When you are on the road to make a big hit.
Commit and go up and get it.
Goals are best when you make a run for it.
Innovation can be exhilarating,
Motivation and big thinking are part of creating,
Have the courage to be the inspiration.
Do epic shit and take a vacation.
Be the spark, when brightening corners of your world,
Your positivity will be observed.
It's always right to be kind and serve,
Shine the light, it's something we deserve.
Learning to change to include "Yes, and."
Thinking through the ask beforehand.

Want to do a good job so things don't get out of hand.
Balance "Yes, and" so that it flows with other demands.
As Stevie Wonder said, "Songs in the Key of Life",
Music has always been my companion,
Never missing a live concert was my pastime,
Music fills my soul and helps through the climb,
Oh, the places in the world we'll go,
The pandemic has made travels slow.
Keep memories of adventures in my mind,
Pining to take a break from the grind,
Looking forward to Europe and having a great time.
Compassion is always welcome,
Serving others is a piece of heaven.
Be the one professing this progression,
Kindness and giving are such a blessing.
Walking on sunshine and today will be just fine,
Sending joy all the time.
Noting beauty while I make the climb,
Celebrating with music and fine wine.
Rocking the decades, learning along way,
Purpose and passion rule the day.
Family, friends, and travel are life's bouquet,
A fine cheese tray and Veuve Clicquot!
26 million minutes is not a lot,
Time is something I really don't want to end.
Loving, traveling, exercising, and being a great friend,
Making an impact is the currency I'll spend.
Speaking out while living cleaner is my intent,
Getting younger as I age will be a godsend.

ADDITIONS:

If you take one thing away from this book, it's to live joyfully and be happy. You are the boss of you and no one else can do that for you. Be you!

Closing and Gratitude

Acknowledgements and heartfelt honesty.

This book was very therapeutic to write. It was written during the pandemic and a very tumultuous time in our lives. Thank you to the people in my life who help me every day.

First, my husband, Mark, who makes things happen in our community and around our house. He makes things so much easier for me. For my daughter, Lily, who lives joyfully every day and does so many kind things for others.

A big thanks to my family in Ocean Springs, including my mom, Marilyn, my dad, Mike, my brother, Mike and my sister, Blake. I love my family dearly and am so proud of the work they do everyday in their community. Also, I have so much love and respect for my nieces, Lindsay and Allison.

Thanks to my dear friends and family, including Karyn and Eric Froseth, Stacy and Billy Gryboski, Kasey and Tommy Gryboski,

Julie and Greg Bowerman, Donna Marie and David Clemons, Kayla and John Williams, Donna and Johnny Heilman, E.A. and Dustin Weeks, Randy Hain, Jason Rollins, Mimi Robinson, Lacy Basinger, Daisy Barnett, Marie Stein, Mia Davidson, Melanie and Bruce Polk, Leigh Herbert, Heidi Hoff, Elizabeth Nesbitt, Alison Avagliano, Nicole Ryan, Terri Lewis, Tami Olivia, Robin Fitzgerald, Peter Bunarek, Maggie DeCan, Ben Deutsch, David and Danica Lewis, Denise and Dominic Mazzone, Julie and John Lynch, Amy and John Skolaski, Lisa and Craig Herold, Paul and Dayna Herold, Rachel Skolaski, William Pate, Judy Trotachad, Ed Baker, Jon Bridges, Pete Krainik, John Wells, Teresa and Dave Caro, Leslie Curl, Ken Bernhardt, Dave Sutton, Dan Hendrix, Lisa Lilienthal, Hala Moddelmog, Kate Atwood, Kat Cole, Rosemary and Jim Hannan, Angie and Jon Naphin, Steve Ethridge, Emily and Steve Bennett, Sue Sullivan, Kim Joffe, Ann and Jeff Cobb, Patti and Jimmy Abraham, Susan Jones, Becky Smith, Debbie Harvey, Dawn Marie Kier, Cindy Sutton, Ami Huff, Joe Koufman, Liz Ward, Ellen Lemming, Kathryn Townsend, Melissa Minihan, Danielle Porto Parra, Douwe Bergsma, John Muse, John Waddy, Abbey Patterson, Della Smith, Steve Behm, Emily Teeter, Chuck Bengochea, Horace Wilson, Louise Mulherin, Jeff Culley, Maureen and Dave Pitfield, Kevin Craft, Moira Vetter, Mike Grindell, Denish Shah, Mike Rotondo, Ted Wright, Cathy Carlisi, Brad Copeland, Mark Montini, Bob Hope, Rebecca Messina, George Bandy, Richard French, Paul Brown, Alex Gonzalez, Julia Lauria, Andrew Vogel, Jason Falls, Sean Halter, Dorothy Miller-Farleo, Leadership Atlanta 2012 (best class ever), Covenant House Georgia, members of AMA Atlanta, Jennifer Morgan, Amy Panessa, Meg McMananamy, Anika Wharton, Heather Michaels, Liz and Mark Stewart, Dr. Roger and Marlene Herold,

Helene Lollis, Laura Guerin, Susan Stuart, Dawn McNaught, Lee Walker, Joey and Beth Bowers, Pat Upshaw-Monteith, Thelma Straight, Wendi Aspes, Mike Pontius, Adam Albrecht, Michael McCathren, Brad Todd, Angie Yarbrough, Amanda Utz, Mandy Muller, Dawn Steed, Heather and Neel Osbourne, Allison Crews, Lesley Andress, Kara Finley, Cathy Walker Vandemark, Polly Traylor, Shannon Pyle, Cathy Hasbrouck, Anthony and Kathy Polvino, the Garveys, and Vincent and Larry Donroe-Wells.

Thanks to the team at HoneyBaked who were more than colleagues, including Linda van Rees, Jim Dinkins, Bill Bolton, Ken Marshall, Steve Johnson, Darin Morrow, Dan McAleenan, Greg Hundt, Jason Simons, Olivia Kaht, Kasey Hadaway, Ward Elwood, Tim Ziga, Ward Elwood, C.J. Cook, Rachel Russell, Ann Marie Jernigan, Danielle Cartwright, Renee Stevens, and Zach Crain. You are true friends and the #HamFam.

A big shout-out to Jeff Hilimire who challenged me to write and served as a mentor throughout the process. And to Rachelle Kuramoto at Ripples Media who gave insights, tips, and challenges to make the writing process better for the reader.

This book is dedicated to the memory of a dear colleague and my best friend at work, Debbie Domer. I think about you and miss you daily. You were dearly loved.

About the Author

Jo Ann Herold

Author of the 2022 book, *Living On A Smile: 16 Ways to Live a Big Life and Lead with Love,* Jo Ann Herold is an award-winning marketing and brand transformation expert. Most recently, she was Chief Marketing Officer for The Honey Baked Ham Company, marking a collective tenure of more than 20 years with the company. Her experience spans iconic global brands, including Arby's Restaurant Group, Interface, Inc., and Tropical Smoothie Café. In all her roles, Jo Ann earned recognition for her ability to achieve strong financial results and award-winning marketing programs that drove sales and profitability.

An unwavering purpose-driven servant leader, Jo Ann has served numerous philanthropic roles, including Vice Chair of the Arby's Foundation, leader of the Georgia State CMO Marketing Roundtable, past president of the CMO Club and AMA Atlanta, Leadership Atlanta graduate, and Covenant House board member. Jo Ann is widely lauded for her service, including being named the National Diversity Council's Most Powerful and Influential Women and earning a Lifetime Achievement Award from the American Marketing Association.

In addition to her contributions professionally and through service to others, Jo Ann is a dedicated wife and mother.

OTHER TITLES FROM RIPPLES MEDIA

Create Transformative Growth

Lead Confidently Through Crisis

Putting Purpose Into Practice

For large companies, following well-established processes is deemed necessary for securing the bottom line. But what happens when pursuing the status quo slows progress or, worse yet, creates a setback? The 5-Day Turnaround offers actionable steps for driving growth by thinking and acting like an entrepreneur, even inside mid-sized and enterprise organizations.

Most leaders plan for emergencies. But when a crisis hits, it brings unexpected challenges. In The Crisis Turnaround, Will and his team navigate disruptions to processes, projects, revenues, and teams that come as the result of an unprecedented event. The book is a case study that prepares readers to thrive in crisis and even emerge stronger.

The leadership classic The Great Game of Business (GGOB) has inspired countless organizations to operate with transparency and rigor. The first two books in the Turnaround Leadership Series introduce the Purpose, Vision, Tenets & Values (PVTV) model. In The Great Team Turnaround, these powerful concepts come together to unlock a team's unstoppable potential.

Delight in Experience and Wisdom

Create a Culture of Innovation

Through stories and simple action steps, *What Does Your Fortune Cookie Say?* educates, entertains, and inspires. Adam Albrecht, founder and CEO of The Weaponry, offers useful ways to become a better professional and human through bite-sized stories, perspective-altering ideas, thought-provoking suggestions, and reliable techniques for personal growth.

While most companies value innovation, their corporate cultures hinder actual solutions from reaching the market. Michael McCathren, who leads the storied Chick-fil-A innovation center, uses research, case studies, and applications to detail the six essential "Ps" of innovation that are necessary to produce and sustain a resilient innovation organization.

Made in the USA
Columbia, SC
24 February 2023

12915136R00113